A GUIDE'S GUIDE TO MEDIUMSHIP AND HEALING

Lorraine Holloway-White

Cover Design and Photograph ©Philip White

Typesetting & layout by Andrew Brenton

Printed by Lulu

OTHER BOOKS BY THE AUTHOR

A Sceptical Medium

A Sceptical Medium 2

My Life – My Mediumship

Are You a Natural Medium – Your Questions
Answered?

Acknowledgments

I would like to thank my daughter in-law Dawn who gave me my first laptop thereby encouraging me to write in the first place and to my darling son, Philip for the design of my poppy logo and book covers.

The next person I have to thank is author of This Last Summer, Tania Tirraoro. I first met her on Twitter and she mentioned she had put her book on a site called, Authonomy. I was recovering from an operation at the time and bored. Remembering I had written a little of something, I followed her lead and put mine on there too. That was on 4th November 2009 – the rest is history.

I would also like to thank Authonomy, the site set up and run by Harper Collins especially for people like me. Their site helps writers to nurture, encourage and support each other whilst giving a platform for growth to people who would otherwise keep their work locked in a drawer or cupboard for the rest of their lives. I owe them and Tania so very much and thank them from the bottom of my heart.

Laurene, Thomas says thank you. You know what for.

Then there is Lulu. Where would we be without Lulu.com? The quality of their books is superb and the concept of the whole thing is one that has opened doors for so many writers to become published authors without the stigma that used to go with self-publishing. By enabling us to show and sell our work worldwide in such a quality way, they have not only given self-publishing respect and dignity, but the writers who use them too. Thank you Lulu and thank you to all of the above people for making me into the respected author I have become today.

With love and thanks to our friends in the spirit world who do more for us than we could possibly know

INTRODUCTION

It has been suggested I put a little information at the start of this book in order for readers to know a tiny bit about me to show what authority I have for writing it and to explain a little about guides/helpers. Further on in this introduction, you will find they speak to you themselves on that matter in better words than I could ever use.

This book is in an easy to read style that will also appeal to those who are not the usual readers of this genre, but who have an open mind. It is an instructional book aimed at improving the standards of mediumship and healing in order that practices used today by some who are unscrupulous may be recognised and stopped. ,It will help all people awaken their psychic ability if they so choose but more importantly it will show that not all people can be mediums.

It is different to many books sold throughout the world today on this subject, because the words come direct from those in the world of spirit. It is they who teach you and not me.

This is a book which, although ostensibly written by me was inspired by those in the world of spirit and is written in their words. This may seem very strange to you and I have to admit that as A Sceptical Medium I find it pretty hard to accept myself. All I can tell you is that it answers many questions I, and possibly you might have, about this subject and does not appear to be biased any one way or another.

Respect is shown towards all belief systems and faiths of our world and even unbelief's. The only bias shown is towards those who wish to do these works for the benefit of themselves only or have closed minds to the ways or beliefs of other individuals.

It is not an in depth study, it is a book that hopes to guide you on the path you may have realised might be for you. It will also show whom these ways are not for. Those of you who go for readings will be helped to see who may or may not be genuine mediums in order that you get a satisfactory reading. Spiritual gifts of the supernatural or paranormal type are not all given to everyone although many say they are. This book helps to show the truth of that statement in the eyes of the spirit world. That does not mean there are not other ways you can help in this work because there are.

I hope those of you who read this book do so with an open and trusting mind and that you find answers to many questions you might have. It by no means covers everything, but it is a start to help guide you on the way. Maybe another book will follow – who knows. I only know I was inspired to sit and type what was given to me and that when I tried to do it at any other time no words would come. You will find the style of writing suddenly changes from me writing to those who have taken me over which will account for the change from first to third person.

I, like you, wait to see what follows.

Lorraine Holloway-White

A little about me

Quite some time ago a friend asked me to do readings at a Spiritual Centre in a nearby town. They were having a fund raising open day and she felt it was time I started to work in public. For many years, I have been aware of my mediumship and healing abilities, but have been fighting against using them due to my religious beliefs and fear of upsetting God, or my Mother who is a strict Catholic and wouldn't like me to do it.

Although on the rare occasion I had done private one to one readings for friends over the years it had been done without much confidence and although the results were very good, I still wasn't sure if I should be doing it. The healing side is a little different as it crept up on me gradually and didn't seem to be something that would offend God. It has been a constant battle of wills within me over many years and the upshot is that I have now come to terms with the fact I am not doing anything wrong as long as I practice my gifts properly, with humility and if they only ever result in good.

After some thought on the matter I decided to take part in the open day and determined that if I was meant to do this work then I would be helped at the time. It was, therefore, with a little trepidation that I arrived and was given my first reading of the day to do. All went well and everyone for whom I read appeared to be satisfied with their readings. The most amazing part of the day wasn't that though – it was when I received a reading from someone else for myself. What I was told in that reading is pertinent to this book so please bear with me while I try to explain what was said.

The medium concerned has a marvellous reputation and I was one of only two people chosen for her to give a reading to that day. As it turned out the other person never had their reading and I was, therefore, the only one she read for. As part of my mediumship, I sometimes receive automatic writing and during one of those sessions, I was told I was to be given a reading in the near future when I least expected it. It was stated the energy around me at the time would be so strong that the person concerned wouldn't be able to pass me over and that they would give me a lot of information which would stun me. Part of this information would be about my future work with the Spirit world. They stated I needed to be given proof that what I was doing was not offensive to God and that it was what I was destined to do. They, (the Spirit world), had spent many years training me naturally and now my work was to start in earnest. Before this could take place though, they were to give me the proof I needed to show me all that they told me was correct and that they were my helpers and not of my own mind.

Not only do I doubt my own ability, but I also question, which is no bad thing, where or whom the information comes from and whether it is accurate. Part of my reasoning is that God doesn't lie and therefore, if what I get is correct and later shown to be, then whoever gives it to me must be of God and working for goodness. Incredibly, the woman who selected the people to receive a reading told me I had been chosen due to the strength of the energy surrounding me and that she had found it impossible to pass me over. That is exactly what I had been told would happen in my automatic writing.

The reading was totally accurate and I received very credible evidence throughout. As part of the reading I was told there is an incredible light shining all around me which draws people to me and not only was my light shining here, but it shone even brighter in the world of Spirit. She said many Spirit people were trying to draw close and I was surrounded by them. She stated I was a natural medium and healer and that I should be working in those fields. The medium also told me that what was holding me back was my worry of offending my Mother and of going against God. She was so right. Here was the proof I had been told I was to receive.

There is no need to tell you too much more of that except for one thing. She told me I was to write a book; the third medium to tell me the same thing over the last couple of years. She also said it was to do with my writings (as I call my automatic writing). This time it wouldn't be exactly automatic writing but more inspired writing. She advised sitting at a computer for maybe an hour each day and then wait to see what would happen. I began by typing in the first person and then it appears as though a helper/guide has taken over. That seems to be the pattern throughout and may explain changes in style of writing that you'll see in this book. So, here we go.

Guide's/helpers who are we? (as now spoken by them in their words)

You will notice throughout this book that we refer to helpers as well as guides. We are aware many of you will refer to us as your guides but this can be very misleading. We do not guide you or protect you in the way your main protector does. There are others whose job it is to do that and our job is different than theirs. We as helpers are of the spirit world now but were once of your world. That is why we understand human emotion so very well. This is why we are able to communicate with you the way we do. We know what humans behave like; feel like and how they are likely to respond to various things in life. We, at one time, had the same feelings and emotions as you. We felt pain, joy, desperation, happiness, sadness, grief, worry, elation and in fact, any emotion you care to name. That is why we are able to help communicate with you in a way you will understand.

Those who we call guides are of a very different nature. They were never of your world and are, therefore, destined to work in a very different way to us. They have never experienced human feelings or emotions and have no real understanding of things beyond what they are permitted to know in order to help you. They know all about you including your inner thoughts and it is they who guide you and guard you throughout your lifetime. They are with you from the moment you enter this world until your very last breath and will do their utmost to keep you safe at all times.

Many people wish to believe and teach that we are all one and the same. This is not true. What many of you call angels do exist and they are not of your world, never can be and never have been. We have heard said that guides and helpers of the spirit world are angels and vice versa. Not true. We are not the same as each other and can never aspire to be.

There are many things in the world of spirit that we inhabit now, which you know nothing of. You are not meant to and should stop trying to say you know exactly what it is all about. You do not and shall not until your time to pass comes to you. It is only then that you shall learn more of the secrets which will then unfold before you. There is a very good reason for this and it is not for you all to question why. Be happy with what you are allowed to know and stop trying to speculate.

We are able to tell you a little for your knowledge but no more. There are many of you who will listen to what we say and believe us. There are many more who will choose to ignore it as it does not agree with their thoughts and beliefs. So be it. We do not wish to make anyone stray from the path they are on if it is right for them in this lifetime. Their time will come to gain more knowledge and understanding and this is probably not it.

So many of your world believe they hold the key and that what they teach and preach is exactly right and the whole truth. This is not so. There is not one living creature of your world who does know the whole truth. Some have some knowledge whilst others may have more. Some of what you think you know will be correct whilst much more will be wrong. It is not for you to know which of these things they are whilst of your world. All any of you need to know is that you must lead the best life you are able to lead. Help others at all times. Be kind to man and to beast. Stop wanting all you see. You are provided with enough for your basic needs and that should suffice. Sadly, for most it does not.

There are those who profess to be spiritual who really are not by any means. They use this word a lot and most have no idea of its true meaning. It is not enough just to read books and want to be different from others. To be a truly spiritual person you need to live the life within and without. Within is more important although many may not realise this. What good you do that is unseen is worth far more than that which you do in order for others to see and know of. All are worthy, but true goodness shines from within. It is this inner goodness for which you should all strive.

The ones we speak of called your guides are the ones of spirit who wish to help you with this. They are the ones who were never of your world and their job is to help guide your path throughout the whole of your life from the second you take your first breath. They will try to steer you away from those things that are bad for you and will try to put you on a path you need to go down. It is often thought of as your conscience. This is in fact your guide trying to help you.

Your guides are also your protectors when you work with us in spirit and with your mediumship; it is they who look after you and keep you safe. Each and every one of you has at least one and at times will have more. This is why we say you do not need extra protection and that it is afforded you automatically. That protection is with you throughout your lifetime. The only time you need to call on more is when you are doing that which is wrong for you or in the wrong way.

Each time you work with us you should say a few words to your guide and protector. You should say you are about to work with those of us in spirit and will they now work with you in order that the best work may be achieved by us all. This is all that is needed. Intent told to them in order that they may stand more on guard than usual. Some of you may call it a prayer if you wish, but it needs only be very simple indeed and does not need to be said aloud.

Please try to remember the differences we have told you. Your guides and protectors are of pure spirit and have never been of your world. They never shall be as the work they do is what they were created for. You may call them angels or any other name you so desire. We call them angels but it is your wish entirely what you call them.

The others who work with you in your mediumship are not guides or protectors they are spirit helpers. We were of your world and as such have not been elevated to that position which you all afford us. We are but helpers sent to assist in the communication between both of our worlds. We are aware that most people will ignore what we say here and will insist on calling us their guides. They will also wish to call us by many fancy names as well as simple ones.

We have no need for names where we are. It is you on the earth who need this for identification purposes. Why do we need that? If we work with you there is no need for confusion. All you need know is that we are your helper. From time to time we shall give a name if there are many who work with you at once. It is still not necessary though as each of us will work a totally different way with you which is what will distinguish us one from the other. We do know that you like names and it makes you feel more secure. It is for this fact alone that we shall at times give a name to you.

We hope this section has helped clear up some questions that we know some of you have regarding angels, guides, protectors and such like. It makes no difference to us what names we are all called by. We shall all do the jobs we are destined for regardless. You will call us by whatever name you choose but we have taught you the correct way, it is now up to you what you choose to do. Be rest assured we shall not be offended whatever you decide. All that matters is that we work well together for the sake of goodness. Talking of goodness, maybe this would be a good time to talk of what else it is we have come to teach you.

What is this book?

This book that we write is not to be an in depth teaching manual about all aspects of spirit work which is why the sections are to be kept brief. It is but a start to teach where those who work today in this field go wrong. Not all people, by any means, are working incorrectly, but sadly far too many are. Due to this, many of the teachers we have working for us today, have themselves been taught quite badly. Like all things in life, bad habits are learned and then passed on to others. It is this that we wish to correct and help with, in order for the standards of mediumship and healing to improve.

Reading this book will also help those of you who use mediums, healers or clairvoyants. We hope to show you which of them appears to be genuine and which ones are best avoided Not only will we give you guidelines on how to distinguish between those who are genuinely gifted and those who aren't, but we shall also give lessons on how your psychic ability can also be awakened and developed should you so wish.

We do not wish to offend the spiritual leaders or churches that teach this work and encourage it to be done; instead we would like to congratulate them. No, what we wish to do is help guide them in the ways we wish this work to be done and by whom. It is through no fault of their own that they are teaching the methods they do. They themselves have been the victims of shoddy mediumship that has been practiced now for many years indeed. In fact, these shoddy ways of practicing and teaching began before your time here now. It is, therefore, not your fault. Please forgive us if we offend, as that is not our intention.

The spirit world is most grateful to those who help us to continue our work and we, in turn, wish to help them. That then is the reason for this book to be written. The one we use to write this for us is herself now learning and is almost ready to work with us. She has, in fact already done many things but has yet to develop the full potential she is capable of. That is soon to follow after this manual is completed. She is not at all responsible for the contents of this book and we use her only to pass what we need to tell you on to everyone. We are most grateful to her also for allowing us to use her in this way.

Please take your time with learning this work as rushing to learn anything is not good. Taking one's time is always the way to work best. For by doing this you will not miss the important things you need to learn and can polish what you do properly. We will follow up at some time in the future, with our instruments permission, with manuals which will be more in depth in each aspect of the contents of this book. This is just to start and make you aware of what is wrong today in the work which is now being done.

There are many good mediums and healers at work throughout your world and for this we are delighted. Our greatest desire is that all aspects of mediumship and spiritual work are raised to the same level. We wish to denounce those who are out to hurt and confuse people with their lies. What we need are the teachers in the world to listen to us and learn. We shall, at some point be writing a small manual for their benefit only. It shall be aimed at the teachers in order to help them learn the correct ways to help their pupils. There shall also be short manuals for all aspects of spiritual work in order that you can all develop correctly and know that what you do is pleasing to God and the world of spirit. If a job is worth doing, then do it well as you say in your world. This is a saying that we too agree with.

By having this book published and sold throughout the world, we hope that the standards we wish for will be raised and met. Any of the people reading this who are genuinely gifted natural mediums will understand and agree with what we are saying. There will be many more who will disagree with most of what we say and we are prepared for that. Many of these people will find that if they are misusing the gifts they have then they shall in time be taken away from them. The work they have now will start to dry up. We shall be blocking these people from carrying on this work in the way they do.

As we have already stated, doors can be opened and doors can be closed. Anything that is abusing the gifts of the Lord is to be prevented from now on. There will always be those who pretend and will confuse and abuse peoples' trust. These people will have to pay for this at another time. All will be judged on what they do in their lives at some point and they are no exception. This book, therefore, is aimed at those who are prepared to listen and learn. The ones who are prepared to recognise that maybe the ways they were taught have been incorrect. It is also for those who wish to understand more of these things that we talk of.

Not all has been wrong. Sometimes it is only small parts of these teachings, which we have to correct and hope they will be willing to listen to us. We do not wish to lose those teachers who have helped us so much in the past and who still do at present. They are too dear to us and very precious. They are the ones we are depending on to help us in our endeavours. These chosen ones are to help shape the way of things to come in the work of the spirit.

We are very excited at this prospect and look forward to assisting you all in this work, which we are to do together. So many more people will be able to be reached and taught the ways of the spirit. So much badness is in your world today and much of it is due to a lack of faith. They have no belief, faith or understanding in anything but the here and now. They are so wrong. If only you all knew what we now know there would be so much less trouble in your world. The Godlessness is what is killing you all and it has to be retrieved.

Too many church leaders of all religions and belief systems are either not doing their jobs well enough or are misguided in what they teach. They need to be stronger and stand firm in their faith in order to show those they guide the correct ways. No one in your world knows the total truth of things and this is only to be learnt on your passing. You shall have many choices to make at that time, but you also have many to make now. What you do and how you decide to live in this world is important to your future. It is the world into which you shall follow on passing from this earthly life that is most important.

It matters not at all what religion you belong to, what belief (or unbelief) system you have or what way you wish to serve. What does matter is that all you choose to do is for good. Follow a path of goodness towards yourself, fellow man and beast. Look after nature and all that you have been given to live with in your world. Those who strive to do good will benefit in time. It is not always in your world that you shall see these benefits, but be rest assured they amass and are plentiful where you next go.

Teachers have a greater responsibility than the rest of you, as their teachings and guidance are what you may live your lives by. They have a huge responsibility and you should be very grateful to them for agreeing to take on this work. Those, however, who teach the wrong ways and are aware that they do so, shall have to be answerable for their actions. These people have misguided many throughout several lives past and present and they are some of the ones we need to teach today. Then there are those who are the victims of the ones who wish to teach their own ways as well as ours. This cannot be allowed to continue if the work is to be done well and accurately. We ask then, that you all will read this book and listen. That you will act upon what you read and try to follow the guidance we give you. Please help us to help you. By doing this, we together, are able to help so very many in your world. Forgive us again for being so brutal but we hope you understand the reasoning behind it all.

CHAPTER ONE

Psychic ability (sixth sense) or mediumship

There are those of your world who say that everyone can learn to be a healer and that everyone can learn to develop into being a medium. This is not so. Due to this most serious of errors, the standards of both have been very badly compromised. This teaching also means that many people of your world are using those who suffer, for their own monetary gain. This we wish to see stopped immediately with your help.

This is a book written in order that all healing and mediumship can be practiced in the most beneficial way to all concerned. At present, many people throughout your world are helping us in our work but not always in the best way possible. This is not necessarily their fault. There are many reasons why this could be and one of those reasons is bad teaching. Let us explain

The ones who teach this belief are mostly not natural mediums themselves but are usually those who have also been taught this misconception by their teachers. If they are natural mediums and still choose to teach the wrong ways then they are not working with us properly. We hope to be able to help guide you in this section about the realities of these gifts, how you will know if you do actually have them and how to understand if you haven't.

If you are born with one, two or more of the spiritual gifts you will become aware of this fact yourself. It will be a gradual awareness that what you see, hear or feel, can at times, be very different from what the people around you experience. This awareness can start at any age. Each person's experience is different from another's. It can be from a very young and early age or not until you are older. Sometimes those with these gifts are not aware that what they experience is different from everyone else but accept them as normal things that happen to everyone. It is only later they realise this is not so.

Maybe this is a good time to mention psychic ability. Everyone of your world is able to develop his or her psychic ability and this is probably where the confusion started. There is a very big difference between using psychic ability and being a medium. We shall explain the difference for those of you who do not understand this.

Psychic awareness is akin to a sixth sense or, if you like, instinct. It is a sense that every person of your world once used automatically. As time passed and man progressed this sense was gradually used less and less. Some still use it today without realising it. You may sense someone staring at you and on turning to look find that you were correct in that assumption. That is you actually using your sixth sense. At other times you may instinctively know what to do. How come? You are using a part of your brain that man long ago stopped using. It is because of this that you are able to develop that part of your brain should you so wish. This is the psychic ability being developed. It will not make you a medium.

When you start tapping into this part of the brain and using it, you will be able to do all manner of things you could not do before. You will start to feel the energy from other people and objects. You shall become far more sensitive to the atmosphere on walking into a room or a building. There are many things you will be able to experience which you couldn't before. This is what is really meant by development and awareness. Today, however, too many are teaching that development and awareness means teaching you to be a medium.

A psychic can tell you things about yourself by reading your energy. Each person, animal or object in your world has an energy field around them. Another name for this is the aura. Living creatures have a more extended aura than inanimate beings. Each living creature's aura or energy field will be different to one another's. Some are very close to the body whilst others extend well away from them with varying levels in between. This aura can also alter many times throughout your life for lots of different reasons; illness, tiredness, awareness, energy and vitality, happiness, depression or any other number of reasons. For those of a good and pure heart it is well developed and open at all times in varying levels. Those of a closed heart and soul will also have a more closed aura that will never extend far from the body unless they undergo a change in their attitudes during their lifetime.

For those of you who have never tried this before there is a little exercise you can do which shows you how to feel your aura. Do not worry if at first it feels very close to your body, this is only because you have not yet developed your awareness. Hold your hands in front of you with the fingers straight out. Face the palms towards each other as though you were holding a package. Now, gently and slowly move your hands towards each other and apart again. Together, apart, together, apart. It should be done several times without ever touching one palm to the other. As you do this, try to sense the feeling in both of your palms at each stage. What do the palms feel like when they are apart? How do they feel as they start to get closer to each other? Do this several times until you feel a pull of power similar to that of two magnets. When you feel a little resistance then you know you have touched your aura.

At first you may not notice anything, but with practice you will start to become aware of what we talk about here. Some people could find this exercise doesn't work for them. This is nothing to worry about. It could just mean that this is not a time in your life that you are ready to acknowledge these things. Maybe in time to come, sometimes not for a few years, you will be ready to try again and find it now works.

This is what we mean by the energy field. It is when you become fully attuned to this aura, or energy field, around other people that you will be able to "read" them. You will amaze yourself at the knowledge you can pick up from reading the aura of a person or animal. We shall speak with you a little later about how you can develop this awareness either on you own or with other people. The people who develop this ability to its full potential are often called clairvoyants. The terms psychic and clairvoyant are both correct for this type of work but they are not necessarily mediums unless they also work with the spirit world – more will be talked of that later. For now, we are explaining only about this book and its content.

We have explained what psychic energy is and have told you that anyone can develop it. We will now explain what is different about mediumistic ability. A medium is always a fully developed psychic or clairvoyant, but will also be able to feel the energy field or presence of those who are in the world of spirit. It will often be felt as a difference in the temperature around them. The air will go colder and can vary in its strength. Sometimes it is a gentle chill but it can also get very cold indeed. The person or people that they feel at these times are not of your world any longer, which is why the temperature they bring with them is different from that of your atmosphere.

As a medium develops his or her ability to tune into those of our world, they will feel their presence much quicker and stronger. This is something that cannot be taught. It is not you who decides whether you are to have this gift. What you can decide, however, is whether you wish to use it. Many of those who are destined for this work will choose not to use it until later in life. This is often due to circumstances around them or because they have not learned to develop it for other reasons of their own. If they have been chosen to receive these gifts you can rest assured that they will work with us at some time or other though even if only for a short while or in a very limited way. Some will work with us very well indeed and others will choose only to do intermittent work with us. They are exercising their free will which all of you possess.

Those who have been chosen will work with the higher and purer energies of our world, which will result in a higher standard of work. Those who try to develop this mediumistic gift by force are drawing on lower energies that are always looking for people to use for their own reasons. Why is it that so many people believe that once someone has passed from your world to ours they undergo a rapid personality and character transformation? There are people of your world who deceive and pretend to be what they are not. They fool you into a false sense of security until it is too late to free yourself easily. The same can be said of the world of spirit. It is these lower energies who work hard to deceive those who wish to learn healing and mediumship. We do not want to upset or offend those who genuinely would like these gifts to share for the good of others. May we reassure those people that, in time, they shall work with us. It is just not destined for this lifetime and so they need to be patient.

There is a way that all of you can tell very easily who is working with the higher levels and those who are not; their personality and character is one of the main indications. By this we do not mean that they will never get annoyed, irritated, upset or angry. They are human beings with human frailties after all. No, what we do mean is that they will be pure of heart. Their only wish is to help others. They are not the ones who are overcome by ego and greed. Their only wish is to serve. You will find that they usually put others' needs well before their own. We shall talk of this at a later stage also and will cover the tricky matter of whether to charge and how much would be acceptable.

We hope in this book to cover most of the questions you may have about our work and will try to break it down into easy to read sections you can turn to at will. Obviously, we cannot cover it all here but hope you find it a good start. There are several sections to be covered and so we shall do our best to explain as clearly as we can in order for you to understand those things that may be puzzling you.

You will find that there will be a lot of people who will try to tell you that we are wrong. That is their choice. It is also your choice what you choose to believe and do in this life. We are only trying to guide you in as gentle a way as possible in order to help you understand a little more about our world and the way we work with those in yours. Every person has a will of their own, and should never try to force their will or opinion on another. If they are truly working with the higher energies and us then they will not do this. They will respect your opinions and beliefs and will never try to force their own on you. They will know that each and every person has to seek their own way on the path of what they believe to be the truth. You will all reach your own destination at the time, and in the way, that it is right for you.

When you pick up this book, it is your choice whether you read it all or not. You may have had it passed to you to read or chosen it yourself. Whatever and whichever way you came upon it, it is your choice what you then do with it. We are here only to guide you and if you choose to accept what we say to you then we are pleased. You may, however, choose to ignore some or all of it as rubbish. That again is your choice and we shall not be offended whatever it is you decide to do. For those who find it of interest, we hope it has helped you along your way a little and answered some questions you may have had.

Earlier we said we are not guides and yet now we talk of guiding you in this book. It may seem to be a contradiction, but it isn't. The way we guide you here is not as your main guide and protector. They will guide you in other ways than we do now. We are guiding you on a path of learning, not on your life path. Your main guide and protector is with you on your life path. These are two very different things, which we hope you will come to understand.

One thing we must say to you. Please do not delve too deeply into all of the mysteries of life (and death). There are many things that you are not to know of whilst of your world and to delve too deeply may result in bad health and mental instability. There are things you can learn and do, but many others you should leave alone. As we have said before, it is not for you to know all things in this life and to try to puzzle over them is to no avail. All you will achieve by doing this is to confuse your mind and cause yourself possible upset. It is relatively easy to know what these things are as you will be able to tell whether it feels comfortable and easy or not. If you feel at all uncomfortable with anything you read, hear or feel then walk away from it immediately.

There are those who will try to encourage you into things that should be left alone. Trust your instincts at all times. All things that come from the world of spirit that are good for you will make you feel uplifted, content and relaxed. You should feel energised rather than drained of energy. You should feel happy and relaxed not tired and withdrawn. Your heart rate should slow and not race. Take note of these things and if there is anything, you do not feel comfortable with, then never be embarrassed or worried to say so. If those you are with accept that willingly and happily then that is good. If there are those who tell you that in order to learn you must do everything they say whether it makes you comfortable or not, then they are not working with us. They are working with the lower energies. Nothing we do with you will ever make you feel at all uncomfortable. - only at peace.

As with all things, there are positives and negatives. Everything of the world has its opposite. The same is of the world of spirit. Where there is good there is also bad. In order to only work with the good then please follow those simple guidelines we have given you. If you only work with the good, you will have no need for protection in a way you may be told. Those who tell you horror stories are the ones who are working with low energies. Walk away from them; they are not the ones who should teach you or help you. A simple prayer asking for good and to be helped and protected is all that should be needed. If you are feeling ill, very tired or low then you must never do this work as your energy levels will be too low and that is when you may be more at risk of lower energies being able to step close.

Whilst you are learning is when you need to be careful. This is when you need to pay extra attention to what you feel and who you mix with. Go only to those who you trust and feel comfortable with. Do not go to classes where you will be made to partake of everything they decide you should. It is your decision what you do and don't do. A good class and a good teacher will always allow you to be yourself and only do those things you are comfortable with. Pick your friends wisely at this stage as it will greatly influence how well you develop as a medium.

Remember, you cannot develop what is not there in the first place no matter how hard you try unless you wish to work with the very low energies we have talked of. Small achievements will not be proof of anything. If you've never had it, you won't get it now just because your teacher says you will. The exercises for awareness are for all people to try as this is to awaken the psychic ability which lies in all of you. From thereon, most of the exercises are for those who are truly natural born mediums or who think they may be and are wishing to develop their gifts with our guidance. It is hoped that any of you who wonder whether you have these natural abilities will be able to understand them a little more. Remember, it is not in depth study, just a book to help guide you on the right path. We wish you well in your studies.

CHAPTER TWO

Awareness - part one
Awakening your psychic ability

Before you start, there are several things you must do. First, make sure that you are wearing comfortable clothing. Nothing too tight or restrictive should be worn. Loose fitting, comfortable clothes that are neither too warm nor too light are best in order that the temperature stays acceptable. You must then turn off all electrical equipment that may disturb you including telephones. If you have any animals or pets then they should be shut in a secure room in order that they cannot get out and disturb you. If you so desire you may light a couple of candles in order to help you relax. Music is not necessarily a good idea although we are aware that many people desire it to be playing in the background. This can in fact, distract you from what it is that we are trying to show or tell you. Peace is the best way to enable your mind to connect with ours or, for those who are not mediums, with a psychic energy.

A comfortable chair is also a necessity in order that you are comfortable throughout the sitting. It is acceptable to eat or drink in moderation beforehand even though there are those who would tell you otherwise. It is not a good idea to do something if your mind is filled with thoughts of food or drink because of thirst or hunger. Nor is it a good idea to overeat. Instead, a good balance should be met. Everything in moderation in life is always a good way to be.

Now we are ready to begin our sitting. Sit in whatever way is comfortable for you. There is no need to sit in any particular way. We have heard said that one must sit with feet placed firmly and square to the floor with their hands on knees and the palms facing upwards; that arms and legs should not be crossed as it will block us from getting through. There is no need for this at all. If we wish to communicate and the channel is clear, willing and able to receive us then we can do it no matter how you are sitting. If you wish to sit with your legs crossed and your arms folded then that is how you should be. It makes no difference at all to the communicator. We are able to give whatever we need to show you or tell you regardless of how you are sitting or what you are doing.

There are times that we shall interrupt what you are doing in order to give an urgent message that cannot wait. At those times you won't be sitting in any particular way waiting to hear so forget all you have heard or been told and just do what you are comfortable with. Being comfortable is the most important thing when you start learning to communicate with Spirit. If you feel awkward or uncomfortable with how you are sitting or behaving, it is this that will block the channel from receiving accurately or in some cases at all.

The reason we tell you to close your eyes is because outside influences can distract you. Should you find this difficult then don't worry. It would be worse to try to force your eyes closed, as this too would distract you from relaxing. Instead, focus on a spot in front of you that feels most comfortable. It is also a good idea to slowly take two or three deep breaths in through your nose and then out through your mouth. This will help to regulate your breathing and relax you. When this has been done, then just sit quietly. Try not to let too many thoughts rush at you or through your head. Try very hard to clear your mind of everyday business and matters and if it helps, then picture yourself sitting somewhere very quiet and peaceful.

It is very important that you don't try too hard at clearing your mind. It is not an easy task and the harder you try, the more difficult you will find it. The very act of concentrating on this will, in itself, keep the mind too active and stop you relaxing. Instead, try to think of something very peaceful and relaxing to you. Each has their own idea of what this is. It could be sitting on a beach listening to the water over the sand or pebbles; being in a forest listening to the breeze through the trees or sitting with a favourite pet stroking them. Whatever works for you is what should be done. Maybe picturing yourself lying in bed sleeping peacefully would help or just looking at a lovely white light.

As you are sitting there allow yourself to feel what is around you. The very air itself – what does it feel like on your face or skin? Can you feel it through your hair? Can you smell it? What does the air smell like? This exercise will help to awaken your senses that you may not otherwise be using properly or to their full potential. The point of this today is not to hear, feel, smell or sense Spirit but to awaken your senses to your psychic awareness or sixth sense. The first time you sit in this way you should set a time limit for yourself. We suggest no more than a quarter of an hour. There is no need to sit any longer than this in order to attune oneself with one's senses. It may take several attempts before you feel you are achieving anything but do persevere if you wish to work well with us.

For those who are natural mediums, this exercise will also benefit them for their future work. In order to communicate with the Spirit world one has to be very sensitive at times to minute changes around them and within them. Without this sensitivity, you will be unable to understand or sense what it is that we wish to communicate to you. How will you know the difference between what you are feeling normally and what we are making you feel?

Too many people today in your world are trying to rush this part of the exercise. Without it, there is no way of doing the job you are destined for properly. In order to work together we must all be able to communicate as best as we possibly can. Anything done is life is best done properly in order to achieve the best results. Many mediums today are not practicing correctly and are, therefore, giving incorrect messages that people do not understand. This type of work is shoddy and should not be tolerated or allowed. We try to do our best with the medium we have but at times, they make our work so much harder for us.

We are always happy when someone from your world wishes to communicate messages for us. It is not enough though just to want to be a medium. Not everyone is able to do this work correctly or effectively. There are people who should be guided by their teacher to seek elsewhere in order to serve. Not all humans are able to work in this way even though many are taught that this is the case. It is due to some people believing this that we have such poor communication with the ones who are being trained by those on earth. It is now time that we showed them how it should be done in order for the standard of mediumship to improve.

The best way to describe to you the difference between a good or poor medium; a natural or forced one is this. Imagine being at a concert where there is the worlds most famous violinist playing a haunting melody on their instrument. He is a naturally gifted musician who was born with the gift of music inside him. He raises his bow and places it on the strings. Immediately, listening to them is making you feel quite moved and peaceful emotionally and physically. You are swept away with the beautiful sounds they are producing which can almost leave you breathless with the purity and perfection. This is equal to a natural born medium who has tuned and developed their gifts over the years.

Now on stage follows another violinist who imagines himself to be just as highly gifted a musician as the one before him. After all, he too went to the best schools and was taught to play an instrument and all else that needs to be taught to musicians. What if they have no natural ability though as the first one had, how will their music sound in comparison? They raise their bow and start to play. The sound is far inferior to that just heard and at times is even scratchy and harsh to your ears. The melody they play may well be recognisable, but it hurts your ears and makes you feel distinctly uncomfortable and on edge. This is the equivalent of a bad or forced medium. One who has not been chosen to do this work, but thinks they can be taught it. There are the differences. Sadly for us, it is mainly the second violinist we see the most of in our work. We wish to see and work with those who are as the maestro. We hope this book will help towards that.

These Gifts of the Spirit come with a huge responsibility, which not everyone is able to recognise. It is not a game and nor should it be treated as one. Many wish to do this work for the prestige, the money or just because it makes them 'different'. Those are not reasons for doing it. Nor is 'just wanting to do it' a good reason. This is probably the time to talk of those who are working with other than the spirit world of which we speak.

There are those who enter into the world of fantasy and not reality as we see it. They talk of all manner of creatures fabled and real. These are not the people who we wish to guide in this book. If they wish to learn about the world of true spirit and mediumship then so be it, but it is not a book for those who seek further afield. For this, they should look elsewhere. Animals may present themselves to be seen in order for the medium to speak of them, but they do not pass messages, it is the guide who does this. Those who speak of such things are not doing our work or with us. There may well be a place and field for their work, but it is not with us and this is never how we would communicate.

The ones who have been chosen to work with us will have been guided to this work throughout their lives. They may have been aware that something was happening to them at different stages even though they may not have understood what it was. Others may not know until a much later age. It is usually a gradual awakening though that cannot be ignored and will not go away. There are those, however, who are aware almost from birth that they have this ability. Those are very rare cases. To all of the other people who wish to work in this field but do not have the gifts of healing or communicating, we suggest that they would be better put to work helping the ones who have been chosen to do so. This is another way of helping spirit and is equally important in helping us to continue with our work.

No one person's work is more important than another's. However you work to assist us, be assured that we are truly grateful and we thank you.

There are many ways of teaching how this work is to be done and not all are correct or incorrect. However, the ways we teach you here are in order that the best work can be done and higher levels of communications reached. It is not written in stone that any one way is much better than another, but this is how we see the best results being achieved. It is, therefore, the way we choose to teach you.

Many times you will need to sit in peace the way we have shown you today in order for the right frame of mind to be reached. It is only time to move forward to the next stage when you know that the peace in your mind and body has been attained. You will be aware of this stage without needing to be told. It will feel different to you from the way you normally feel. Only after attaining this level are we then ready to move forward with this. It is now time to go on to the next stage.

We wish you to be with another person of your choosing for this next part of the exercise. It should be someone you trust and who can respect what this work is about. They too should be trying to reach the higher levels of communication that we teach you now. You can choose more than one person for this but only two of you should ever sit together at one time during this early stage. Maybe you can swap partners for the first few times this is done. Eventually, you will all come together to do it as a group.

If you are truly naturally gifted in this field, you will be drawn to the person who is to take part in the exercise with you. When the choice has been made, then a time and place equally comfortable to you both should be arranged for the next sitting to take place. It may be an idea to keep to the same place and time each week wherever possible, as this will make you more comfortable.

We are now ready for the next phase of your development to begin. Make sure you are both comfortable in the way, which was spoken of to you earlier. When you are both ready and prepared then sit as before and close your eyes. This time we wish you to become aware of the person with whom you sit. Be aware of their presence and note what you are feeling.

This exercise will take slightly longer than the previous one, as you are now to feel changes within and without another being. Take time to adjust to the quiet space and peace as you were taught before and only when this state has been achieved may you move forward. When you have reached it, you may then move your senses to become aware of what surrounds you. Notice what you feel and acknowledge all of the things your senses are conveying to you about the immediate space surrounding you. Once you have done this extend your awareness beyond that space and allow it to go towards your friend.

Stay within the quiet and allow yourself to feel the energy surrounding this person. Do not yet attempt to go within them or to read more than you need at present. Just to feel a different energy than your own is enough at this stage. Whilst doing this you might become aware of many things surrounding that person. It could be colours, smells, a strong energy force, varying emotions or total calm and peace. Whatever you are feeling you should try to hold those thoughts. Hold those feelings and become familiar with them. Do not try to reach beyond them at this stage. If you feel yourself beginning to go beyond that then bring yourself back immediately to the place of peace within your own energy field. Once your peaceful state has been resumed, then you can reach out again towards your friend.

You will know when the time feels right to bring yourself back to the present automatically. When you sense you have felt all you are going to be able to without going any further then you can bring yourself back. At all times during this exercise, you must feel calm and peaceful. If at any time you feel uncomfortable or your heartbeat quickens then you must cancel the exercise and leave it for another day. If you have chosen your partner well then this should not happen. It is only when one of you is not pure of heart and has the wrong intention that this exercise will be of any discomfort. If this uneasiness persists on further sessions then you will need to change the person you sit with.

It is not necessary for you both to finish at the same time, as each of you will feel different things at different stages. If you are to return to awareness before your partner then sit very quietly in peace until they too open their eyes and return to their normal state. As before, set a time limit for this exercise. Usually about twenty minutes will be enough.

When you both feel ready, then it would be a good idea to get out of your chair and have a little walk around. At this point maybe a cup of tea or coffee or any soft drink of your choice would be appropriate. This is to enable you to come from any altered state in which you may or may not have been. Take your time with this, as there is no hurry.

As with all exercises of this kind, you will find that you may go into an altered state. This is not possession, nor is it trance. It is only a peaceful state of mind similar to a deep meditation. As in anything of this kind, it is never an idea to pull yourself back to the harsh reality of day-to-day living too quickly. Allow your body and mind to adjust slowly.

When you are both ready and feel fully 'awake' and alert then sit together and share each other's thoughts and feelings. Let one speak at a time and share their thoughts and feelings with the other. When they are finished then the other may share their findings too. After each has spoken of what they experienced about the other, they should then discuss it together.

One might find that they experienced far more than their friend did or maybe neither experienced anything. It might take a couple or a few attempts at this exercise before anything at all is achieved. Remember, every person will move forward at his or her own pace. You must also be very honest when discussing what you felt, and the one listening should never take offence or be afraid of what they are told. Those of us in the world of Spirit would never wish to upset or worry anyone of your world. Interpretation of one's feelings is not always correct, and it will take time before it is perfected.

It is also difficult for those of you who still exist on your earth to understand some of what you might feel and to be able to put it into words that can be understood by others. Some of the feelings you experience will be beyond the understanding of your world and are but a glimpse for you to experience what lies beyond. At these times, you may have great difficulty in explaining *how* you feel or *what* you felt. Eventually you will know you are unable to go further with this exercise and it will then be time to do this with several people at once instead of individually.

If you have been lucky enough to have done the first part of this with several friends individually then now may be the time to ask them all to sit together. This will then become a home circle, which should help generate far more energy and opportunity to experience more. I ask you not to take things any further at this stage but to keep it as you have been doing. For now just do the exercise as before and feel each other's energy fields. Discuss your feelings with one another, at first individually and then as a group.

You will become aware that people have their own unique energy field surrounding them. Familiarise yourself with each persons. Compare them all – how do they feel and how do they differ from each other? Due to the fact that there will be more of you doing this exercise it would be an idea to limit the time taken on individual discussions in order for each of you to share your experiences. Repeat this exercise weekly until you all feel that you are unable to experience more without going further. It is important that no one tries to rush this stage. As with all of the stages we shall take you through it is important that each one is experienced fully in order that the senses are awakened properly. It is after this that we will be able to take you on to the next stage in this development.

These stages of awareness are really for those of you who have not progressed on your own. Although capable of learning through experiences given to you naturally by the spirit world, some may feel inhibited or unsure of allowing things to 'just happen' whilst on their own. There are those who feel more comfortable going through these early stages with others who are at a similar level. For those of you who are already very aware then you can obviously skip these stages if you so wish.

Do not have too many people in any one group or it will be impossible to sit and do this exercise properly. You need time to feel everyone's energy field and whatever else you may pick up from them. In order to give each person the time needed to do this it is necessary to limit the numbers taking part. We would suggest no more than six to eight people. If there are many friends involved then it may be sensible to form two groups who could then mix about from week to week. However you choose to do this it is very important that this stage is not rushed and that every person feels they have achieved their full potential. It is only time to move on when the very last person is ready to.

Also, if you are interchanging the group, then it is important that the energy is still comfortable and good. If the balance changes then you will need to keep swapping people around until you reach the correct balance. This does not mean that one person or other is a bad person, it is just that some energies connect far better and stronger with some than they do with others.

Each stage you reach teaches a different process and none of these should be rushed. Every person will take a differing amount of time to reach his or her full potential in each field. Not all will be able to achieve this in every exercise as not everyone is blessed with all of the varying Gifts of God. Some have one, others one or two and yet others again may have all or most of them. As we have said earlier, there are also people who have none of the supernatural/paranormal gifts but they are instead gifted in other fields.

Due to the fact that so many of you are at varying levels of development, it is most important that those less quick to develop are given the time they need to progress at their own pace. If it is found that some are taking much longer than the majority of people in the group then it may be necessary to form a second one. If, however, it is only one person who is not progressing at the same pace then maybe they would be better having one to one tuition or waiting till another time as maybe they are not quite ready to progress at this stage of their lives. Those of you who have successfully completed the first part of the awareness exercise are now ready to move on to the next stage.

CHAPTER THREE

Awareness – Part Two
A little psychometry test and the responsibilities
in mediumship

We have now shown you how to feel the energy field around yourself and other people. What we wish you to do now is feel the energy field around different objects. This is an easy exercise in psychic work and will not take quite so long to achieve as you are now more attuned to your senses. It is a pointless exercise to feel furniture and soft furnishings in a busy room as there will be too many conflicting energies connected to each item for the beginner. It is therefore, better that you start with an object worn by another member of the group.

In order for this to be achieved effectively, each person should remove an item and place it on a tray in the room. This should not be done in front of each other. Preferably, it will be done in a separate room and when all items are present then one member of the group should bring the tray into the room. It is a good idea for one member to sit out of this experiment in order to supervise. The following week someone else may take their place in order that they too can take part.

Once all of the items are in place, the tray should be offered to each person individually and one item they feel drawn to removed by him or her and held in their hand. It is obviously not a good idea to have anything too large in order that each item may be held easily. It should also be said that the item people place on the tray should not be anything that very obviously belongs to them. If the object in question were to be recognised by others in the group, it would affect the outcome of this exercise. It is therefore vital that no one knows what belongs to whom.

When you have your chosen object, do the exercise as before. Be aware of any feelings you may be receiving from the item you are holding. Take note of anything you feel or smell. Are you getting any pictures in your mind, names, or knowledge of any sort? Remember everything you experience. Maybe none of you will feel anything to start with. It may take a few attempts before you feel anything at all. It could well be that none or only one or two of you will gain anything from this exercise. Not all of you will be able to do it, as it might not be for you to do in the future as all people will work in a different way to each other. It is very easy for the imagination to work overtime during this task and it is, therefore, better not to say too much to start with. Sometimes people will experience a smell, sensation or other feeling and not realise that it is from the object they hold. In the early stages of trying these experiments, the signs might be very subtle and, therefore, go unrecognised. After several times of doing this exercise you will start to recognise the subtle changes though so do not worry if at first you appear to experience nothing.

When it is time, the person leading today's group will ask each in turn to state whether they felt anything. This should be kept brief. Anyone in the group, who is genuinely gifted mediumistically, will be aware if the person speaking is passing knowledge received psychically or if it is from their own mind or imagination. Once each person has spoken and related their experiences, then the object's owner can tell them whether they were correct or not.

This should always be done truthfully. Never should anyone lie and pretend that people have correctly given information if this is not the case. Nor should what is said ever be altered to fit what others want it to be. Sometimes those learning may be tempted to do this. It may be they want to spare the other persons feelings or they might think this is helping to encourage them. This is something that is done by less scrupulous people and it is one of the things that gives mediumship such a bad reputation. If anyone in your class or group tries to do this, they must be stopped immediately and informed that this is not acceptable behaviour. If they were doing it to be kind, they must be taught that it is not kind, it is how bad practices are formed. Nor is it helping the other pupil as it gives them a false sense of their true achievements.

Spirit never lies. We have no need to. If we give information to our channels then we always give them the truth. How that person then interprets what we give them is important. They must never be encouraged to improvise or add anything else to make it sound better in their psychic work or it will only lead to those same practices being adopted in their mediumship later on. Give only what you receive and no more. A psychic reading should be conducted in exactly the same way as mediumship. Honesty and integrity are very important in this field of work. Having an open, honest mind, heart and soul is an absolute must. Without these, the purity of what we try to achieve is missing. If you all learn at these very early stages of awareness to work honestly, then we hope that you will continue to do so throughout your work with us later on.

Sadly, not all who read this will be one hundred percent honest in the information they impart to others during the years they do this work. The temptation to astonish and astound those who come to them will, at times, take over. We do not do this work to astound or astonish anyone with grandiose statements. What we do is bring comfort and hope to those who are still of your world. We wish to impart a little of what we already know to be true to the people of your world. You who are mediums are instrumental in helping us to do this work and grand statements or behaviour is not how it is to be done. Respect and humility are key requirements to our work and we ask you to keep this in mind at all times if you wish to continue on this incredible journey that we take together.

We have tried a little psychometry and now maybe you can practice linking into someone's energy field (aura) in order to try telling them some things about themselves. To do this, pick a person from your group who you feel most drawn to. Hopefully, they will be drawn strongly towards you also. Find a quiet space where you can sit facing each other and make yourselves as comfortable as possible. It should be decided who is to talk and who is to listen. This will most probably cause quite a few laughs at first and even some embarrassment. Take it in turns. Maybe five minutes each to start with.

Look at the person in front of you and try to clear your mind as much as possible. If you feel something, or if a thought comes into your head say it. When you first try this, you will probably feel quite inhibited and it will mean that you are not relaxed enough for it to work properly. After a while, you will find that you start to feel more comfortable. Once that happens you will find that you relax far more and this, in turn, will enable you to be successful.

Some will only ever be able to do this exercise psychically but this part of your awareness is what could start to awaken what has lain dormant until now. It is once this part of you has been triggered that you will be ready to start linking with spirit if you are meant to. Again, we ask you not to rush this part of things. Be content to practice this at length. Try it with as many people as you can for now until you become very accurate and learn to distinguish between information given and your imagination or own thoughts. We will be talking to you later on about linking with spirit and how you will recognise the differences between psychic and mediumistic work.

We ask you at these early stages of learning to be very careful what you say. There are things that may come to you that could easily offend or upset others. These can be thoughts that have come from your imagination or just plain old mind tricks. When receiving something that could be deemed to be of a sensitive nature, hesitate. Wait awhile before saying anything. Dismiss the thought from your mind and only speak it aloud if it keeps coming back and will not go away. If you are meant to impart upsetting details then do so with as much tact and diplomacy as possible.

There will be times through your years of working with us that this will happen. These early stages of practice with your friends are the times you can make mistakes. These mistakes are what will teach you how you should be saying things to others. It will also teach you that there may be some things better left unsaid. Never should anyone be upset or angered by what you tell them.

Much of what we teach you is to enable you to grow. It is not only in order to help others and to bring them comfort. You also need to learn to grow within yourself in order to move forward and progress in the next life you shall live. It is not necessarily a life in your earthly world, but could be in the world of spirit. This is a decision that shall be made later and is not one to worry yourself over now. It is a decision you make when your time to leave this earth you live on is at an end and you prepare to move forward. Then shall you be asked what it is you wish to do with your next life. It is not a matter to be concerned about before this time. It is though, something you should now be preparing for.

Within the life you lead now, there is great need to be ready to learn what lessons you came here to learn. Many of them shall be very hard indeed and others easier to bear. Each and every thing that you experience is to teach a lesson and better your chances of progression next time 'round. Not all chances offered to you will be taken and shall be ignored or not recognised for what they are. It is these times that will have to be repeated at another time or place. Maybe some of these chances will be offered to you at various stages within the life you lead and live now, whilst others are wasted opportunities never to be repeated in this lifetime. Not knowing which of these is which, means you have to be very vigilant indeed. Make sure you are aware of all that you are and all that you do. Sometimes you will be aware that you have missed an opportunity for learning a lesson only when it is too late. This need not worry you as the very fact you recognise this is in itself a lesson learned.

People can come and go throughout a lifetime and all will have a lesson to teach you. Not all of these are good experiences but they will enable you to grow if you recognise them for what they are. You will find that the people you meet throughout your lifetime are at different levels of spiritual awareness. Some will not be as aware as you, some may appear completely unspiritual, others will be about the same level as yourself and yet others will be far more advanced. Each of these people has a lesson to teach you in their own way. Remember, it is not the good times where you learn your lessons it's the bad ones. Therefore, each bad experience you have to suffer in life you should actually say thank you for and be grateful. They are the ones, which help you to progress quicker on your spiritual journey and make you who you are today.

Those with less spiritual awareness will need patience and understanding from you, as many of them may not have progressed beyond the materialism of the here and now lifestyle. They are unaware of any existence beyond what they see in front of them in their everyday lives. They are on the very first stage of their journey through life. As a being who has progressed further, you should always show understanding and love towards these souls. They have a very long journey ahead of them with many pitfalls and you, having come into their lives, have a very important role to play. How you behave and respond to them could mean the difference between them progressing or staying at the place they are now.

Those of you who are more spiritually aware have a very important role to play in life and a great responsibility. How you are and how you behave can influence others who watch you far more than you realise. You may be held responsible after passing from your world for how you influenced others. Lead by example at all times. Try very hard to be polite and caring. Show love to others whenever you are able. Extend the hand of friendship to all who you meet. Help where help is wanted, show care where caring will make a difference to those who need it. Your life whilst on the earth you live in is very important indeed. It will define how and when you shall progress further and whether that progression is to be within a further life spent on earth or one spent in the world of spirit.

A reckless thought or word can make a huge difference. Most of you are unaware of the impact your very being can have on another soul. The simplest of things said or done without thought can make a huge impact on another person's life. It can decide whether that person is to progress or not. By your example so others may follow. At all times try to be aware of your behaviour and think how it may influence another person.

This is the hardest job you shall probably have in your world as the way others treat you can also influence your behaviour in return. It is a circle that is never ending. The greatest lesson you as a human being can learn is how to overcome all negative attitudes. Turn them into something positive. Do not allow these negative thoughts, words or deeds allow you to react in a bad way. Use them as a means to grow in your awareness. Let them be the hurdles and steps you need to further your progression on the spiritual ladder. How you react to these people or situations will either help you to grow or hinder you on your spiritual journey. How you react, and are seen to react, shall also influence others who watch, especially those who are the perpetrators.

The important lesson for you to remember is, not only are you a pupil in this life, but you are also a teacher. The whole purpose of being is to grow and help others to do the same. Your progress will depend on how willing you are to learn the lessons put before you. At many moments throughout your life, unexpected things will happen or occur to upset the balance of your day-to-day living. How you cope with these moments will establish the extent of your growth and development. Some of you will cave in and give up, others will plod through trying to cope as best they can, whilst others again will treat it as the learning curve it is and embrace it.

Each problem or upset that has to be faced in life will be treated differently. Some will be far easier to handle or cope with than others. There are some which will affect those close to you and will, therefore, be very difficult for you to accept or even understand at times. Life is not meant to be easy and the easier it is then the younger the soul experiencing it. The harder life becomes, then the older and more advanced the soul who experiences it probably is. Each and every living soul is given experiences that they need to face up to. Some have far more than others and the older the soul the more they have to cope with. They are able to bear more as they have a deeper understanding of all things spiritual and the necessity of what they go through. It is they who have the greatest responsibility of all.

It is their behaviour which will influence those they meet, favourably or otherwise. They must be aware at all times how their behaviour influences those around them. There are those sent to make this task much harder and each lesson has to be faced and learned before they can move on to the next. At times this will appear to be unbearable and even unfair, but it is all for the good of the soul bearing it. In the order of things, it is necessary for this to be done and borne. It is said that no one person shall be given more than they can bear. This is very true and even in the case of suicides that occur, due to the pressures and upsets of life, this can have been the way that person's life was meant to go. It is only in very few cases that the person concerned cuts off their life before it is their time.

It may appear to those of you reading this that what we have just discussed with you is not part of your awareness. It is actually a very important part, if not **the** most important. Without any understanding of others' problems or difficulties and without any compassion you will be unable to do the work you are destined for. These are the fundamental things required for a person to be the best medium or healer there is. There are those who practice both healing and mediumship, but lack the basic requirement of compassion. These are amongst those practicing today who we wish to see stopped. They are amongst those who give mediumship the bad name it can have amongst the sceptical.

Compassion, understanding, caring and a desire to give as much as you can of yourself to help another human being is a very basic need for one who wishes to serve others. For serving others is exactly what mediumship and healing is. It is a service to one's fellow human beings. Once this has been achieved then you are ready to start developing your mediumistic abilities. Until this is the case, you should not attempt to work with the world of spirit.

In some cases, this will never happen in this lifetime. There are those who think themselves compassionate and caring and yet come out with some very scathing and cruel comments to, or about, others. They talk of their looks, body size, and general way of life and think it is their right to pass comment and judge that person. It shouldn't matter to those who serve what a person looks like, behaves like or what their belief system is. If you wish to serve, you do so unconditionally and your heart should be in the work you wish to do in order to serve that person well. If you are unable to do this without judging them then this work is not for you.

Just because you don't voice those thoughts aloud does not mean they are not there. If you think these things even to yourself then you are not ready to work with spirit. God never ever judges by one's looks or manner of dress or by where they live. He judges by what is in one's heart and soul and this is what you too need to learn to do. This usually only comes after many years of hardship and suffering on your part. That is why so many healers and mediums who practice well, are in their later years. There are odd exceptions where a younger person has achieved this state, but it is usually only in one's later years that this is obtained.

This again explains why so many who work with spirit have exceptionally difficult lives. Health problems, injustice, cruelty, money worries and all manner of things can be theirs but they persevere. Most people in life will become hardened and aggressive due to this whilst others will grow in understanding and compassion for those who suffer similar fates. It is very easy for one to think that the world owes them something and say "why me". It is very hard to accept hurt, injustice, constant ill health, money worries or similar problems and not complain. It is those who do not question why all of these things happen to them who are actually the survivors. They are the ones who learn and grow from these life experiences. They are the ones who have been guided to the path of healing or mediumship that will do the best work.

You see they never ask "why me?" They ask instead "why not me?" Why should it be someone else? Why would you wish what you are suffering on another? For by saying "why me" you are, in fact, wanting it to be someone else who suffers instead of yourself. They never judge a person on looks. Instead, they have compassion. You don't know why a person looks or behaves as they do. What may be wrong in their lives? What has caused them to become this way? Without knowing their life or experiences you have no just cause for judging them. God is all-knowing and He doesn't judge a person throughout their lives, instead He tries to help and guide them the right way and forever prays for them. It matters not what they do. He and the entire spirit world continually pray for lost souls or those in despair. Until the day each and every one of you dies help is extended to you.

This then is how those who wish to be effective and accurate mediums and healers must be. If you are not of this train of thought then you are not ready to work with spirit no matter how much you may desire to. Yes, you shall be able to attain small measures of contact or results, but they are not the results that we in the world of spirit wish to be related with. You will be working with those lesser spirits who are not always working for the good. No matter how well it may appear at first things will always deteriorate.

To work with the highest and the best the medium should also be of the highest and best. To work only with those pure of heart, you too must be pure of heart. Whatever your failings in life are, so too will those failings be of the ones in spirit you attract to work with you. Remember, like attracts like and if you are attracting the wrong spirit then you need to look within yourself. God and the world of spirit are never wrong. Do not question them if things go wrong. Question yourselves. It is within you or your heart that the fault may be found.

Many reading this will disagree and it is those very people who are not ready to progress. If they cannot understand or see the truth of what we have just told them, then their eyes, hearts and minds are closed to the truth and they are not ready to work with us. If you need to work hard on protection with strange rituals and imaginings, then you are not working the correct way. If you only work with the highest and best, that protection is afforded you automatically.

If you are disturbed in any way by bad experiences then you have either not yet progressed far enough to do this work or you have a bad teacher and should change where you are training. The majority of those who try to force mediumship and learn it are the ones who suffer from this disturbance. Those who have been chosen to work with us for the sake of good will probably never have experienced anything of this sort and never shall. This is a very good indication to those of you reading this as to whether you have been chosen for this work or not.

There is strange talk of overshadowing and being unable to breath. This is where a bad entity comes too close to you and can cause fear and disturbance of the mind and body. If this ever happens to you, then you are allowing them near to you by trying to do those things you shouldn't. Stop trying to be a medium, it isn't for you. You are bringing those bad energies upon yourself. If you still continue after this warning then it is your fault if you suffer. These are the people who must **never** be allowed to do readings or healing for others. Sadly, many are.

For those who have learned the necessary lessons needed to do this work properly the only protection needed is a short prayer. If your prayer asking for help whilst working is of pure intent then that prayer is answered. Faith at all times is all that is necessary. Ask and believe that you have been heard. If you believe this to be so then you must also know your prayer has been answered.

CHAPTER FOUR

Protection

This section and some of the following chapters of instruction are for those who are to do work in mediumship. Everyone can read this book as it will help you all to distinguish who is and who isn't working properly and with the highest and best. There are also further chapters which talk of things that all readers can help with and do. Any development from now though, is for mediumship and not psychic ability. Those who are psychic cannot do these things unless you are mediums. We have already said about those who force them to happen and have no need to repeat ourselves. All mediums are psychic, but not all psychics are mediums. Even if you are not to aspire to mediumship in this life, you will find the following chapters informative and of interest.

This is to be a very brief section indeed. It is the question of protection. So many people of your world are obsessed with strange rituals and cantations all in the name of protection. How they came by these strange ways, we do not know. It has become quite out of hand and we have watched it grow over many generations with amazement. There is definitely need for protection when doing this work as there is in all ways of your being. What there isn't a need for is such drastic and dramatic behaviour.

If anyone of your world works with spirit then they need to be careful. However, this said, let us get it in perspective. As in all things in life, there are opposites. So it is with us. Where there is white, there is black. Where there is good, there is bad. Where there are good spirits, there are also bad spirits. In order for you to be protected from these spirits who wish to cause upset and mischief, it is very important to be of a pure heart when working with us. This is why we wish to teach how this should be done and by whom.

Those who are forcing trying to learn these gifts are the ones who attract the wrong kind of spirit. For the rest of you who are chosen for this work there is no problem. If you continue to work in the way shown to you by us then you have no need to fear. A short prayer is all you need to say at the start of your work. This can be said in any way you like. It can be a prayer taught to you as a child or it can be a prayer you have made up. Any words at all will do. All that is necessary is that you work in the way we have taught you through your life.

Those who work with us, do so with a pure white light. It is the purity within this light that keeps you, and those you work with, safe from harm or disruption. The ones who are not chosen to work with us do not work within this light and can cause upset in their own and other peoples' lives from mischievous spirits. To be pure of heart and of pure intent is what is needed. The one we use to write this book for us has a prayer, which is said before she works. We shall give this prayer to you at the end of this section should you wish to use it. It is one that was said by many in years past but has since been forgotten by most. It is a prayer to Saint Michael who protects one and all in both our worlds.

You will probably find that as you progress more in your spiritual life that you change quite considerably. You will become more selective in those you socialise with in order to keep good energy around you at all times. In order that those spirits who you wish to avoid cannot come close, you will instinctively start to avoid people to whom they attach themselves. You will probably not be aware of this at first, but as you progress through your awareness and development, a change will overcome you. These small ways will show you that you are indeed working with those spirits of the higher realms who only wish to serve well.

You will begin to notice other changes in your life and others who know you will also see these changes occur. If you wish to follow this path then change is inevitable. You cannot develop properly and start to work with us if you retain the materialistic views of the secular world in which you live. You will rise above all of that and start to see the world and those who live in it with different eyes. Your purpose and needs in life will also start to change. If you note these changes and they happen to you for the better then you are most probably on the right path.

Those who are on a similar journey will recognise in you that which they too are striving towards. You will be drawn to each other like moths to a flame. Likewise, there will be many more who profess to be on the same path but who you will cringe away from. This is the true definition of discernment of spirits, which you read of in your Bible. As your awareness grows and we continue to work together in a pure way, your intuition will become more astute. You will see the true purpose behind most who call themselves mediums.

Your very purity of heart and willingness to learn from us rather than your earthly brothers is why you are protected from harmful spirits. Stay on the right path and you will have no need to fear. We will watch over you at all times. Call upon us to help if you are concerned and we shall show you the way. True faith and belief in goodness can work wonders. Whatever your belief or unbelief is, it is important that you always have faith that there is one (or something) far greater than you who watches over all things; who sees all that takes place and acts upon it when necessary.

We do not mean that this book is the only way in which you can learn. When we talk of your earthly brothers, we mean those who intend well but teach the wrong ways. By reading this book, you will be able to find which teachers of your world are working with us and which ones aren't. You will be able to discern which teachers work with the higher energies and which ones are struggling to work with those from lower realms. Many of the others mean well but are to be avoided at all costs if you wish to work properly and safely.

Be rest assured my friends that we watch over you at all times. Do as we ask and guide you to do and there will be no need for worry. We now will give you the prayer that we spoke of earlier together with another you may prefer. There is no need for you to say either of these prayers if you do not wish to do so, but they have helped many in the past, especially the one to Saint Michael. There is no need to say this aloud, it is sufficient to say it in your mind. Nor do the people who you read for or heal need to say a prayer. It is for you, the one who works with us.

The second one is a prayer you may prefer which is to your Guardian Angel. Every living person has one appointed to be with him or her for the whole of their earthly lives as we discussed earlier in the book. You may call them by whatever name you prefer, but be assured, all of you has one with you at all times. They will never interfere but will try to gently guide you on your way and help wherever they are able without altering your destined path. The first prayer covers all eventualities. Even if there are those who do not believe in the devil, they know there is true badness out there and it needs to be protected against.

Prayer to Saint Michael
Saint Michael, Archangel defend us in battle
Be our protection against the wickedness
And snares of the devil.
May God rebuke him we humbly pray
And do thou O Prince of the Heavenly Host
By the power of God
Thrust into hell Satan and all evil spirits
Who wonder through the world
For the ruin of souls.
Amen.

Guardian Angel Prayer
Angel of God
My Guardian dear.
To whom God's love
Commits me here.
Ever this day
Be at my side.
To light and guard
To rule and guide.
Amen

We hope that one of those prayers may help you. If you do not want an Orthodox prayer, then as we have said, any words will do. We will say however, that the prayer to Saint Michael was once widely said throughout the world. Once this was stopped, the world began to change drastically for the worse. Anyone who checks back on this timing will see the truth of that statement.

The above prayers will give you a guideline on what is needed. We would be very surprised if the ones chosen for this work did not believe in prayer in some form or other, as they will be well aware that there is one far greater than they are. It is His work that they do. If your intent is pure and you only work with good then no harm can befall you or the ones you work with. Good cannot hurt and nor does God. There is nothing more pure or good than God and if this is Who you work with then nothing bad can hurt you or be allowed to come close to you. We hope you now realise the futility of strange rituals and hope you will feel sufficiently secure that your work with us is safe.

One last word on this matter; you will at times be at a social occasion when we call on you to pass a message or to help someone. If you have had a couple of alcoholic drinks, it matters not. We would never call on you to serve when it was inappropriate. We are better judges than you of when are the right times for a message to be passed. You will not draw on bad spirits by doing this when you have had a drink or two. We have heard many of your world say this is what shall happen. The only people who will experience this are those who are not working properly in the first place. Trust in us at all times as we too are placing our trust in you. If you have concerns then it means you are not working in the right way. If you are working correctly, as we have said before, you shall feel comfortable and at ease with what you are doing.

By having a drink or two we do not, however, mean several. Never try to work when you have over indulged as to do so would put you at risk from mischievous spirits. The reason for this is because your guard will be down and your ability weakened. They will see that you are not being vigilant and will try to creep in the back door. Although we have said that there is no need for extra protection, we do expect you to be vigilant at all times when working with us. Your ability to work with the light and remember to say your prayer is impaired when in a drunken manner. Even when one works with the purity of heart needed, there is still a small risk of disruption.

You will not be bothered by true evil, but there will be those who wish to try to deceive with falsehoods. It is, therefore, very important to test the spirits at all times. Never be too trusting. If you have doubts about any information given, then you are undoubtedly being fed falsehoods. That is the time to tell that particular spirit to go away. Refuse to work with them as their only intent is to deceive. You may find as your mediumship is in its very early stages that this may happen from time to time. It is only because you have not developed the confidence and ability to discern bad from good yet. It will only feed you lies though so there is no need to fear of anything worse.

If ever a spirit of mischief approaches, a true, fully developed medium who trusts in us will always be aware that something does not feel right. Trust in this instinct at all times. It is these times that you are being guided. Be very aware, as falsehoods will often be mixed in with the truth in an attempt to put you off your guard. It is for this reason that you need to be alert at all times you work. Do not be too concerned if you realise that you have been misled at some time. This is not a reflection on you or your mediumship. It is but another lesson you have learned from.

It is also another reason why it is good to take your time when reading for someone. Rushing in with the first information you are given can often lead to error. Test all information before you pass it on. Only pass on that with which you feel truly comfortable. If you have any doubts at all then it is probably for a very good reason. If in doubt, don't pass it on. If it is correct, then another opportunity will present itself at a later date for this information to be passed to the person concerned. The important thing is to try to be as accurate and honest as possible. Be alert, have faith in your work and us. By only accepting the things that make you feel comfortable and that you do not have doubts over, will ensure your mediumship remains pure.

If teachers talk of putting bells, glass boxes, reflective mirrors, blankets, cloaks or any such other nonsense around yourself for protection, then they are not the ones who we wish you to work with. We are hoping that by now, having read this far, you will have started to realise that these are some of the strange ways we talk of that we wished to see stopped. There is no need to say more on this subject and so we now move on to a subject where our work is most needed.

CHAPTER FIVE

Healing – who can and who can't

W e wish to speak in this chapter about healing and the differing ways it can be done. The purpose of this section is to talk to you in more detail and explain those ways; how they should be done; what you might feel; what the other person may feel; and what outcomes to expect.

The first thing to tell you is that only those who have been afforded this most special of gifts will be able to help us to heal another person. Nobody can be taught to heal as it is not something that can be acquired. All gifts whether of the spiritual or human have to be given in order to be received.

Let us give you an example of what we mean. There are five main senses afforded to humans of your world. Of these senses, not all people will have each of them. Some people may have only one or two whilst others will have them all. They are given in varying degrees however your Creator sees fit.

It might seem very unfair that some are born with no hearing, no taste, no sight or any of the other senses. Those who are born without some of these senses are the ones who are least upset by it. It is others who tend to feel what they see as the unfairness of it all. You are wrong to feel this, as you know not why this has been done. How do you know where this stands in the fullness of time? It may well be that this is needed for a specific purpose for their needs in the world they enter after the one they live in now.

Those without are the ones who accept their lot and realise that there is nothing they can do to change it. They get on with their lives and usually will outshine others in various ways as they compensate for whatever it is they lack. For example, one who cannot see will usually have an extraordinary sense of hearing far more developed than any of those with all of their senses. This could mean that they can shine in the field of music for example as their hearing is finely tuned to hear what others cannot.

Someone else with no sense of hearing may well develop an extraordinary sense of smell. They, due to this, could shine in the perfumery world for example. Discovering and creating new and exotic perfumes that people will rush to buy. Those are just a couple of examples, but they are intended to show you that not all of you have the same gifts or talents in your life. They are all given to you or withheld from you for a purpose and this is not for you to know of at this stage.

You should never question what the Creator has destined for you. Accept what you do have and make the best of it. Use those gifts you have been given and make the most of them. There is much you can do with the talents you have. Too many people of your world strive for what they can never have and ignore those things they do.

It is all for a purpose and those of you who strive for things you shall never be able to attain delude yourselves. Sadly, in your attempts to try to practice the spiritual gifts you also end up letting down others who place their trust in you. This is very wrong. You must accept the facts as they are presented to you. There are talents in life that you are able to learn and attain, but the gifts from God cannot be learned, they are given.

You could all learn to play an instrument for example, but only some of you will be able to take that further and become sought after musicians. Most will be able to just about hold a tune if they are lucky. You can also be taught how to read; something, which no one can do at birth, but can learn as they grow and progress. These are talents that one and all can learn to a certain degree. As we say, some will excel, others will be mediocre and yet others again will be somewhere in between. Those who have been given the gift of being a natural musician are the ones who shall be the maestro's. Those who just wish to learn to play shall not. They will be able to achieve small amounts of ability but not the heights of the naturally gifted.

It is not so different with the supernatural or spiritual gifts. They are the gifts given to some according to their destiny in this life. Some will have a unique understanding of others and how they feel without any outward sign being shown. They will automatically know how to speak to and help these people. Acting as counsellors without even being aware that this is what they are doing. This cannot be taught by anyone. Why are some people so kind hearted naturally to one and all? Why are others seemingly completely uncaring of other peoples' feelings?

There are people who will do anything at all to help a fellow human being or an animal. There are others again who wouldn't care at all if they saw a fellow human or an animal suffer. These people have different characters and natures and they cannot be taught how to change them. It is something deep within that person from the moment they are born.

Throughout their lives, people will change due to many experiences they go through. Some will become hardened by their experiences, whilst others who experience the same things, will grow in understanding and compassion towards others and wish to help them. Why is this? Some people will deliberately be cruel throughout their lives to others be it to human or animal. Others again will do everything they can to aid and be kind to them. These are just a few examples of how each and every human being in your world is different to one another.

All of you accept these differences in each other. You all know that there is kindness in life and there is cruelty; there are those who suffer badly and those who don't; highly successful people and those who will never reach such heights in their chosen professions or careers. We could go on and on showing you these differences in people but have no need. You are all well aware of what it is we say to you. Why is it then that so many of you think you can learn those things that are obviously not for you?

Those who do not have the supernatural or spiritual gifts will be aware of this fact. They may want to have them but know they don't. Why do they insist on pretending they do then? Why do others insist they can teach them to attain them? We do not understand this at all. Why do people strive so hard for what they know they can never attain? The most important question is why do they pretend to others they can do things they know full well they cannot. They are aware when they take money off people for readings or healing that they are not able to do it. They copy what they have seen others do and talk in generalisations that can fit anyone's life.

We know the answer to this. It is because some want to help others. They have a genuine wish to help in whatever way they can and hope to be able to do so in this way. We are sorry but you shall never be able to. Those who teach you that you can learn to do it all are wrong. There are so many other ways your compassion, kindness and caring could be put to good use. Please use the gifts that you do have in a way you are able and stop striving for that which you cannot do. By trying to work in the wrong way you achieve nothing and it means the gift of caring you do have is not being put to use at all. You can still help others but not with the spiritual gifts. Maybe this will be meant for you in another lifetime but not the one you are in now.

We have to tell you all of this because there are many people of your world today who believe that they can give you these spiritual gifts. They believe that everyone has them and that their skill can bring it out or develop it in you. This is so untrue. Why do these people think they know everything? They should know by their very efforts that many of those they teach are doing nothing at all. They must know that there is nothing there in most of these people. If they do not know this, then they themselves are not gifted in this way either.

To pretend you are a healer and can help those who suffer is so very wrong. Do they not realise the damage they could be doing to others by this pretence? Not only are they unable to help the ones who suffer, but by their behaviour and lack of morals they have caused the work of genuine healers to be ridiculed by many. It is due to them, that a lot of those who could otherwise have been helped have not come forward for fear of ridicule.

We hasten to add that not all of these people are frauds and fakes deliberately. Some may genuinely feel they are able to help. The unscrupulous, or just ill informed teachers, may have told them that all people can heal. They will pretend that it is working when it isn't. They lead them into a false sense of security and then let them loose on the world. This is not the fault of the pupil and it is not they who we decry. That said, they must be stopped from doing this though as their lack of ability is adding fuel to the fire. It is only by using genuine healers that respectability and acceptance of this wonderful gift will be attained.

We know many are offended by what we say, because they believe themselves to have more knowledge than those in spirit. They feel themselves to be experts in the works of the spirit. They aren't. No person of your world is. There are those who do good works and have many excellent results in the fields in which they practice, but as we said before, there is only one who heals and it is no one of your world. There is only one who can allow the things you do to be performed, and again, it is no one of your world. You are all instruments and it is decided who shall and shall not be chosen to help us in this work by one other than yourselves.

Those of you who wish to do this work for other reasons than compassion and caring would never be suitable anyway. Sadly, there are a lot of people like this. We know of so many who wish to be healers and yet they have no compassion in their hearts or souls. They care not truly for other people or their worries but are drawn to healing for what they perceive to be its glamour. They feel it makes them special and sought after. A sense of self importance is what they are seeking and it is the ego which causes this.

Ego is a human frailty, which many possess, and it will not help you in your endeavours to develop any of the spiritual gifts, especially not healing. To enable your development in this field you must be ready to put the needs of others before your own at all times whenever possible. How many people do you know who are really prepared to do this? Not too many are there?

The ones who have been chosen for this work, have been picked for a very good reason. In fact, there are a lot of reasons for their having been chosen. They will have lived many lifetimes and will have suffered greatly through some, if not all of those lives. They will have learned many lessons that you have probably yet to learn. The life they lead now is probably full of many problems for them and even their own health can be bad.

Some who read this book are undoubtedly destined to be healers in this life whilst many more are not. You will most probably be aware of who you all are. Some may not yet be very sure but by reading this book, we hope to clear up any doubts you might have. Both those who believe they can heal and those who are not sure can have these doubts. There will possibly be others reading this who are healers and are helping others already. This will only be of general interest to them and may not necessarily teach them more than they already know now.

We hope that this section has helped clear up any doubts you may have about one's ability to heal or be taught it. Please ignore those who say we are wrong. They will try to insist that you can be taught and in doing so, you may well attract lower energies again. Any work of the spirit is not without its dangers and pitfalls. It all has to be done with the highest amount of integrity and only by those who are pure of heart, mind, body and soul.

Those who wish to practice this gift may well find that you can make things worse instead of better. If you attract the wrong spirits who wish to mislead this is a distinct possibility. This is not a game and should never be treated as one. We shall now go on to tell you how this most special of gifts can be done and for whom.

CHAPTER SIX

Prayer for all and absent healing

This chapter shows how all people can pray for another in order to help without being a medium or healer. It also teaches visualisation techniques that again all of you can try to do.

The first way everyone can help another in this life is through prayer. You do not have to be a healer yourself for this purpose, but it is something that is open for all to do. All that is needed for this is a belief in one greater than you are. A belief that there is a Creator who hears all prayers and answers them. As we have already said, healing and prayer may not be answered in the way you wish it to be but rest assured it will be given. It is not always apparent how one has been helped initially, but God never ignores an honest request.

A prayer offered up for you or on behalf of another is always heard and acted upon. If the one offering up prayers is asking with pure intent and a love for the person required, God will always answer. He never ignores one of His beloved children. If, on the other hand, one offers up a prayer which is scornfully said and with no faith or belief whatsoever then it shall probably go unheeded.

There are many people in your world who do not believe in anything but what they see in front of them. It is this that stops them from learning the lessons they are here for. They do not believe that healing can be done or given by anyone but a man or woman of science. How sad this is. To have no belief in anything more than that saddens us all. There is so much more that could be done for them and those close to them if only they were to open their hearts and minds.

This said, it does not mean that those who do not believe in a Creator or any more than the here and now are not to be helped. That is not the case. Of course they too shall be helped if it is so destined as others may offer prayers for them. They need not be aware that these prayers are being said on their behalf, but it often happens that way. It is the person who offers up the prayer or request who is listened to. As long as they have belief and their prayer is true, pure and for the love of another it is heard and acted upon. This then, is a form of healing of which everyone of your world can partake. It is one form that is open to all, the only requirement being that of faith.

There are many ways to be able to help heal another. The way we have just talked of is prayer but it could also be classed as a form of absent healing. Those healers amongst you will already be aware of this term but many will not be sure what it is or what it means exactly. All of you may also be unaware that each person has this ability in order that they might help others. All that is needed is faith. Let us now tell you about it and how it can be done.

Absent healing is a term used by those who are instruments for this purpose in your world. It can be done by using prayer alone or by prayer and visualisation. There are also some who will use visualisation without using orthodox prayer at all. Any way of doing absent healing is actually a prayer although they may not realise it. Those who pray for themselves or others are doing so in the orthodox way, which most people understand and do. There are many who do not use prayer though. Not all are of a belief system where there is a Creator or prayer, but if they have a belief in something far greater than anything of your world they too are acknowledged and helped in their work of trying to help others. They will work in another way, which when used with faith is also effective.

Absent healing can be done many ways depending on the one who is doing it. It can be visualisation of the person who needs healing. Visualisation of the part of the person who needs to be healed or by any other manner of ways they choose to do it. Those two are the most common though. This form of healing can be done by mediums and healers, but more importantly, this is one type of healing that any one of you can try to do.

As we say, there are many ways but we are here to tell you now, which of these is best. Both of the ways we have mentioned to do with visualisation are good, but they must both be done with prayer in order to have more effect. Good intention is always the key factor to any form of healing as is a wish to help the one who is suffering no matter which way that might be. We shall now instruct those of you who wish to work in this way how best it can be done.

For those amongst you who are mediums, if you are also a practising healer, you might be approached and asked if you will help to heal someone who lives very far away from you. This could even be in another country. For those of you who have never been asked this before and possibly never heard about it do not worry. It is very easily done. The best way is to find out the information about the person concerned such as their name, where they live and what is wrong with them. A Christian name will suffice, as surnames are not necessary.

It is not actually necessary for you to have the other information either as we shall be aware of that person's needs just by the fact that it has been discussed with you and you are being asked to help. The reason for knowing these things is that it shall help you and not us. Once these facts have been relayed to you it is then up to you when you wish to start. As we have said, this is something that all of you can do and not just the mediums and healers amongst you.

It is always better to do it when you know you are least likely to be disturbed. If it is not an urgent request then it is probably better to leave it until the evening when all is quieter. Sit quietly in whatever room you feel most comfortable in and where you are least likely to be disturbed by anything or anyone. It is usually a good idea to start with a simple breathing exercise in order to relax you.

Take a deep breath in through your nose, hold it and then let it out slowly through your mouth. Do this three times with your eyes closed. You will find that this will help relax your mind and your body and will regulate your breathing. Once this has been done you are ready to start your visualisation. As we have said, you will all no doubt have your own way of doing this and this is only a guide for those who wish for it.

Keep your eyes closed and try to visualise the person concerned before you. It matters not whether you know what they look like as all you need to do is visualise either a male or a female. They are best thought of either sitting relaxed in a comfortable chair or lying on a bed. Once you have this in your mind we ask you to surround them in a pure white light. Not a light as you would know it but an ethereal light with no hint of colour. It should not be full of glare just a pure white light.

As it surrounds them you can then focus on whichever part of their body or mind is upset or injured. Imagine that light pouring into their body. It is seeping in through not just their heads or any other part of them but it is seeping into their very pores. Each and every pore is filled with this pure white healing light. It has now entered the body through the pores and is going even deeper within them right to the very heart of their body. It is reaching every part of them. Nothing is left un-penetrated. It even goes into the blood, the bones and the bone marrow. It is being circulated throughout the whole body in this way.

As it passes through the skin and pores you'll be aware of the glow still surrounding them but this time more gently. The white light that was surrounding them is now within doing the work it is meant to, leaving behind in its place a soft luminous glow. Whilst you are visualising this you should offer a prayer asking for help. Ask for what it is they require and if they can now receive that help if it is in their best interests. That part is most important.

The reason for this is because it is not always in their best interests to have all manner of pain, illness or any other problem completely removed. It could be that they need to go through whatever it is for their own growth and good. If this is the case, they shall still be helped but it will be in another way. It could just be that they will be helped to accept whatever it is that ails or befalls them.

Sit quietly for as long as you feel necessary for this visualisation to have helped. When you feel that enough time has passed, you will probably be aware that the light and the glow has disappeared and that the person now looks like any other again. This means enough healing has been sent and it will carry on doing its work for as long as is needed. You may do this more than once if desired, but there really is no need to do it daily. The very fact that you have done this and offered the prayer of request is enough for us to do our work.

We carry on doing what you have helped us to start and the only reason for repeating this exercise is sometimes for the benefit of the patient or the one who requested it for them, as they like to know something is being done. Now and then it might also be necessary to repeat it at a decent interval of time just for a top up. It depends how serious the problem was to start with. Obviously the more difficult or serious the illness or injury is then the harder the work to be done.

After you have finished this exercise remember to always say thank you. Everyone likes to be thanked and we in the world of spirit are no different nor is God. Many people of your world are very good at asking for what they want but very few are good at saying thank you. It matters not whether you receive what you want or not. The fact is you asked and were listened to and therefore, it is polite to say thank you.

Acceptance is also necessary. Never question why. It is not for you to know why and by that very question you are showing a lack of faith. In order to do this work you must have faith at all times. Trust in God, trust in us and above all believe and trust in yourself. You can do this for others, anyone can. This is not something limited to those who have been chosen to be healers on earth. This is something that every living person can do if they have enough faith and trust. Remember, another great requirement is love. Love for your fellow human and a sincere wish to help expecting nothing in return.

On talking of expecting nothing in return, remember please that there is to be no charge made for this or any other type of healing. We will later discuss the topic of charging but covering costs for healing is all that is acceptable. Never charge for that which is meant to be given freely. There are some who find it difficult to receive without giving something in return, in these cases they can be allowed to leave a donation of their choosing, but no set fee is to be made or taken.

Absent healing and prayer incurs no costs whatsoever so there is never an excuse for charging for this type of healing. Anyone who does so must be aware that whatsoever you sow, so must you reap. What you do unto others may be done unto you in return.

We have talked of absent healing and the power of prayer, which any of you can do. We now wish to talk of the ways of healing that are practiced by mediums and natural healers only.

CHAPTER SEVEN

Mediumistic Healing
How can you tell if the healer is naturally gifted?
Tips for both healer and patient

This is a way of healing where a medium is used as an instrument in order to help others. There are various ways they work, but we shall tell you how it can be done and what to expect from it. Many people in your world today are helping us to heal others with all manner of ailments. There are many more in the world who pretend they can do this and these are the ones we would like to see stopped.

For some strange reason, there is talk of certificates for healing in your world today. We cannot understand this. It is said that these certificates show the person is a healer and has trained to be one. It shows no such thing. As we have already explained, no one can be taught this – it is a gift. The greatest healer whoever lived in your time was Jesus. It has been proved that he lived of your world and did these things. He had no certificates. He went on no courses and he made no charge. As a true healer's gifts come from the same place that His did, why do the people of your world still insist on these strange things that prove nothing?

A true natural healer has no need for any strange rituals or cantations. Nor do they need to breathe very deeply continually whilst giving healing and get you to do the same as you receive it. We have seen many strange practices carried out by these people as they breathe deeply with their eyes closed whilst making the one who seeks help do the same. You will be made to sit with your eyes closed throughout the 'healing' session. There is talk of chakra cleansing and all manner of things. They achieve nothing at all except a dramatic show for those who want it. If, for example, you come with a bad back, they insist on going all over the body and doing strange things saying that your chakras are blocked and that is the reason for what you are suffering.

This is total nonsense and is why we need to teach you the patient, as well as those who practice healing what is correct. There is no need for all of this behaviour at all. It is for their benefit only as it makes them feel important. In many cases, it is doing these strange rituals that enables them to charge a lot of money. Those who go to them are awed by the wondrous things these 'healers' appear to be doing and the knowledge they profess to have. They are fooled into thinking that their whole body has had a good cleanse. We tell you now, it hasn't. If you have a bad back, then it is the back that we help with. There is no need at all to go to all of the rest of the body unless there is another problem elsewhere.

They often say they must have total quiet whilst they are doing the healing. There must be no background noise or talking anywhere around them. Again, we tell you this is nonsense. It is obviously better to have the healing done somewhere that is not too noisy, but it can be given anywhere at all. If it makes the patient feel better and more relaxed to sit with their eyes closed then that is fine. They should not be told they have to do this though. The healer is able to talk to them throughout and you, as the patient, can talk to the healer. It will not stop healing from being effective.

There is no need for music, candles, incense sticks or any of the other things that people use. If these are used strictly for relaxation purposes then this is fine. We have no problem with that and these things can help to relax the patient. It adds a certain ambience and atmosphere to the room, which can aid in their relaxation, which in turn can help with the acceptance of the healing being given to them. It is not and cannot ever be necessary in order for healing to take place though.

There are those who say that doing all the above things helps give healing and that it cannot be given without these aids. There are even some who profess certain inanimate objects give the healing to the patient rather than the healer or those who work through them. Sadly, there are too many who believe this to be true. We wish that there were none at all of this belief. It is but a means of helping the one giving, and the one who is to receive, by creating an air of calm about them. It is no more than this. If used in this way there is no problem with it at all. As we have said, this can help in the act of healing only by helping the patient relax enough that they can have the faith to believe what we do together is to be beneficial to them.

Depending on where the problem is within the patient, they should sit, stand or lie. It matters not to us only to you and the one concerned for your and their comfort. Also, it is very important that you are able to work where needed. We would suggest that a third party should be present if at all possible in order for nothing to be suggested at a later date by the patient. At no time is there ever any need for hands to be placed on private parts of the body in order to heal. If anyone should try this with you, leave immediately.

Not all are of good scruples in your world and it saddens us to say that you who work with us need to be protected. It is not the dead who hurt you, but the living. They are the ones you all need protection from. The healer needs to be sure that a patient cannot afterwards go to someone and pretend the healer acted inappropriately. Likewise, the patient needs to be protected against those unscrupulous few who prey on the unsuspecting and use healing as a cover for other deeds. It is a sad fact of life this can happen from time to time. Luckily, it is very rare that we have seen this occur. Do not let it put you off if there is no third person present as it is not always possible for this to happen. We just want both healer and patient to be aware. As with everything in life, caution and preparation is always a good thing.

There will be some who come and do not believe you can help them. As you are aware, not all can be helped in the way they wish if it is not destined for them. Some of these people may set out to destroy your reputation. Of those who can be helped, and are, there are a few who will also not be of good character and will set out to hurt you. The ways that these people go about this is varied. There are those who will just try to discredit you and say you are a fraud. Others will say you have made their problem worse and that you have hurt them. As we have already discussed some, luckily not many, will try to pretend that you acted with them and touched them in a way that was inappropriate.

These are the reasons you need to be safeguarded. It is very sad that there are people such as this in your world, but it has to be so. Due to this, please try to do as we say for your own protection and work with someone you trust to be with you. There are those who talk of needing insurance. We can see no need for this and if you work in the correct way this should not be necessary. If it makes you feel better then that is a decision only you can make. We do not see the need for this and if you are not working in the wrong ways then it should not matter.

Now we come to the ways for this work to be done. There are those amongst you who are able to find the problem without being told where it is. If this is the case then it can help to give the patient confidence in your healing ability. For if you can find the problem with no guidance then surely you can help with it. What you must never do is tell them what is wrong. It is not for you to do this. Some 'diagnose' the problem and say what is wrong and even recommend pills, lotions and potions to take. You are not medically qualified - you are but an instrument being used to help us in our work.

There are those who think that 'diagnosing' is clever to do and makes them sound qualified and expert in their field. This is what must never be done. You must also never tell a patient to stop taking any medication they may be on, nor advise any for them to take. It must be stated at all times that they should see their doctor, or if they are already seeing one that they should continue to do so. We cannot emphasis this point strongly enough. There are people today diagnosing and advising about medication and that is why there is a need for some of you to have taken out insurance. We state now, this is **not** healing done with the world of spirit. Nor is it natural healing as given as a gift to a natural medium. These are practices carried out by those who wish to be seen to be important and different. Walk away immediately.

What you and we do together is complimentary to conventional means. Miracles can be achieved if so destined but they are by no means guaranteed and it is a gravely serious matter to tell anyone at all to stop taking medication, start medication you have told them to take or to advise stopping seeing any medically qualified person. There are those who say herbal or natural remedies are alright to prescribe – they aren't. How do you know if they will react with any medication people are already on? You don't is the answer even if you believe you do. Those of you who do any of those things should be stopped and reported immediately. We would be quite happy to see any of you in trouble for this practice as it goes against all we try to do. It is the ones who do this without being qualified to do so that we wish to see stopped from practising.

True healers would never do these things if they were genuinely working for the good of the world of spirit and those we try to help. Even some very good healers though have sadly been attracted to a glamour sometimes afforded to this work. When this happens and they are feted too often by those they have helped, their ego can take over. This is when the problems start. They begin to believe they can do more than they are meant to and start to diagnose, prescribe or similar. This is highly dangerous and not only are you playing God you are playing with peoples' lives. Their lives are not for you to play with. If you start this behaviour, you shall have to pay for it later in this life of yours or at a later time in another. Remember, everything you do in this life has to be answered for at some time.

We may be repeating ourselves, but we cannot impress on you enough that you are only an instrument. Humility is a key word to your success in the field or fields you work in. The gifts you have been given can so easily be taken away if they are abused by you. Any person who is to work with us is at all times to remember that this is work done by the Grace of God for the good of others and not yourself. It may help you to advance in your spiritual life but only if it is done properly and with the humility it warrants.

Now we have spoken to you of the pitfalls of this work and the rights and wrongs of how it is to be practiced, it is time to decide whether you work with hands on the patient or hands off.

CHAPTER EIGHT

Hands - On Healing

How it is done and what the patient can expect

Now we shall speak of healing by the placing of the hands on the body. This is the way that most will probably do their healing at some time or other. It is by no means necessary to do it this way at all times. The way we speak of here is but a guideline of how this may be done for those who are unsure. The ways of doing it can vary depending on what ails them and whether there are problems in more than one part of the body.

We would suggest that all healers would do well to start and finish their healing by the placing of hands gently on the patients head if this is possible. Trust your instincts on where the hands should be placed one either side of the head, one on top and one further down nearer the nape or both hands together on the top. It matters not. What does matter is that you and they are both comfortable with it. We suggest the head as a place to start, as healing being given by us is then able to reach the whole body from here. The patient will usually be aware of any illness or pain they know to be wrong with them, but there may be other possible problems that have not as yet presented themselves. By the placing of the hands on the head, we can then also assist with the other possible problems not yet known of.

The whole of the healing process can actually be done by doing this one thing, but for the patient to feel confident it is often done by concentrating on the afflicted area or areas. In order to instill confidence in the patient of your ability to heal, it would be a good idea to start by finding where the problem is. For those of you who are able to work this way and to find the problem this would be the time to do it. You will each have your own way, but the way we suggest is by running your hand or hands over the aura keeping them approximately four to six inches away from the actual body.

For those who do not know how this is done we shall now explain. By doing this exercise you may well find that this is something you are also able to do but were unaware of until now. You should stand beside the patient and, as in all forms of healing or spiritual work, offer a small prayer asking for help and protection. When you feel ready, you may start to run your hands over the aura. Usually you shall find that only one hand is the one which "finds" the problem. Experience will show you which is which. As each person works in a different way it will be for you to discover yourself.

You will know if you are to help in this manner by what you feel. You will also know which hand is the one to find problems, or if it is both, by working in this way. If you feel nothing at all in either hand then this probably isn't how you'll work. It might take a few practice go's to discover if you can or can't do this as the sensations felt are not always very obvious but can sometimes be quite subtle. They are never however, subtle enough that you need to imagine you feel anything.

We now tell you of the sensations that you might feel. The one most usually felt is that of heat. As the hand runs slowly across the aura, a small change in temperature may be felt in your hand. It is an idea at this point to say nothing but to continue moving your hand slowly around the area and then come back to that part. Is the temperature change noticeable only there or everywhere else. It can be your imagination so you must be very sure by continuing to move around until you are positive that the temperature is indeed different in that one section. The heat you feel in your hand can be from very subtle warmth to a quite intense heat as though a radiator is burning through their skin and warming your hands.

Continue through the whole of the body starting at the head and moving through to the toes. Once you have finished then you shall either have located one or more spots which feel different or you will have noticed nothing at all. When starting out in this field, we recommend trying this on friends who do not tell you what ails them and see if you can find their problem. This does not work on problems such as diabetes or any other illness or disease, which is not located in one particular spot. That is seen another way which we shall talk of later.

Other feelings you may experience are cold spots, which are very obviously much colder than the rest of the body temperature. These are usually located somewhere around hot spots. A hot spot can be where the pain is felt but the cold spot can be where the problem stems from. That is when people suffer from referred pain. An arm may have a problem near the top by a shoulder, but sometimes the pain can be felt in the wrist. This is but an example. These feelings of heat and cold can change. For some it shall be the other way around. Only you can know which is which when you start to use this gift. It will be by experience that you begin to understand the different meanings, which are individual to you. As we have said, not all mediums work the same way, but they do work by the same rules of the Universe and of God.

At other times you could feel tingling or a prickling in your hands or fingers. A type of magnetic force is another means of feeling and finding a problem. All of these things might mean there is a problem in the area you feel it. These are the areas you need to work and concentrate on. You will receive confirmation from your patient if your findings are accurate and that you have indeed located the precise area or areas.

Do remember that you must not try to diagnose or say what you think is the matter. Even if they press you and ask you to hazard a guess you must not do that. Nor must you worry anyone with being over dramatic or by playing up to what you feel. Always make sure that the person concerned is seeing a doctor if you are concerned and never perform spiritual healing in place of conventional medicine. For small problems it matters not but for anything more you should always advise they see a doctor or if they already are then state that they must continue to do so.

As we said before you should never prescribe. Some healers might feel it is acceptable to prescribe or suggest natural remedies. This is not so. Many natural remedies of your world do not agree with man made medicines and can cause ill effects. They can stop their medicines from being so effective or can heighten the effects thereby making people seriously ill. It is, therefore, vital for your own protection as well as theirs that this is not done.

Once these preliminaries are over you are now ready to commence with the healing session. There is no time limit set on this as all healing sessions are different to each other. Some will need only five minutes whilst others can take much longer. You will always know when to end a session of healing so do not worry.

For hands on healing we have already said to start at the head if at all possible. If you are unable to touch that spot for any reason then hold your hands around the aura of the head instead. You will instinctively know when to move them. From there you will be guided to the part or parts of the body afflicted. You may place your hands gently on the affected place and keep it there. You might feel any of the things we have already mentioned such as heat or cold. Whilst giving healing it is usual to feel heat. It is usually quite an intense heat, which will be felt by both yourself and the patient.

When you are trying to find the problem, whatever sensation you feel will appear to be coming from the patient; when you are actually giving healing this changes slightly. It is an almost imperceptible change, which you may or may not at first notice. This time, the heat is from your hands and the patient will usually be very aware of it. Again, with experience you will become aware of these changes in sensation and whether the heat or cold comes from them or you.

When healing is being given, you or the patients do not always feel it in the way we have described above. Sometimes it is a case of trust. There will be no feeling in your hands and they will not feel heat, cold, tingling whatever. These are the times when you must learn to trust that healing is still being given. There are many things that can go wrong with the human body and not all means of treatment are as you would expect. We work in different ways as you are well aware and it is, therefore, not always obvious that anything is being done to help. Time will always tell. When this happens you will not be aware when you have given enough healing. It is these times that you must learn to trust us and your instincts. We shall always let you know when enough has been done on your part and that you can remove your hands.

It is important to tell your patient at the start and again at the end that it is not you who is the healer. Give credit where credit is due. You are but an instrument and if they choose to believe you it matters not. What does matter is that you give due credit to the true Healer. You must also tell them that there is no guarantee that they shall be helped in the way they wish. This is an ideal time to tell them that they shall always be helped when they ask, but not always in the way they want to be. Help them to understand the workings of the Lord. Help them to understand the other ways in which healing may be received. It is not always physical but can also be mental. At times if it is needed it shall be both.

To help you understand what we mean by this we shall give an example. There could be a patient in a lot of pain due to a cancerous condition or some such other illness. They might come to you as a last resort hoping for a cure if or when they have been told there is no hope. The wish on receiving healing from you is obviously for a cure. This may not always be possible if it isn't part of their life path. They will still be helped though and these are the things you need to point out to them. They could be cured or they might just find their pain is relieved and becomes bearable, it may even disappear altogether. In other cases neither happens, but what they could receive instead is an acceptance of what is to come and a peace which they never felt before. Their mind could be given the healing instead of the illness.

When there is very serious or terminal illness involved, it is often an idea to give healing to those who look after the patient as well. They too are often suffering in silence with the strain and upset of it all. Who can they turn to? They may be struggling to cope with the enormity of what their loved one is going through and could do with some help themselves. At times, a whole family could be given healing to help them come to terms with what is to follow. It is amazing how often this can bring about a sense of calm, acceptance and peace to them also.

Please remember when the session is over that you must say a prayer of thanks. When you have finished your work, ours continues. Healing continues for as long as it is needed and does not stop when you take your hands away. Sometimes the patient will continue to feel a warmth in the place you have treated and this serves as a reminder to them what has taken place. A change may be noticed almost immediately whilst at other times it might take twenty four hours before the changes start to be noted. It depends on the condition, the severity and also whether they are meant to be helped in that way at that time. It could be that many sessions are required. Each case and patient is different and you will know automatically who needs what treatment.

There are times that you may hear the problem had become temporarily worse after treatment. This is not too often but should be warned of. There is not anything to worry about with this as there is nothing you have done that could possibly cause any problems. It might be that the area you have just given healing to may have an underlying infection or similar. As with anything of this nature it has to take its course. Before an infection can heal it needs to reach its full strength, so to speak, before it starts to improve. This is what is happening after healing. The healing given is just speeding up this process so that the problem reaches its full height before being healed totally. This may seem very complicated to you but fear not as it is all very simple to us.

It is when doing this hands on type of healing that you shall feel mainly heat or cold in your hands. You can also do healing without touching the other person at all. Sometimes you might feel drawn to use both ways. When giving healing without touching the other person, you will be able to sense more feelings than just hot or cold temperatures. We have already discussed what some of these might be; tingling, prickling sensations or magnetic forces are just some of what you may feel. There are more but these are the most usual.

As with all healing, you will be drawn to the place you need to start and will be guided throughout where you need to go and for how long you need to do it. The usual thing is that when you hold your hand over the area to be treated you will usually feel some sensation in it. At times this sensation may be very intense indeed whilst at other times it could be barely perceptible. You must keep your hand over the area being treated until this sensation or feeling goes from your hand entirely. When all feeling is as normal you know that enough healing has been given.

As before, the patient may continue to feel warmth in that area for sometime after the healing session has finished. Often up to several hours has been noted. Whether you are practicing hands on healing or just placing hands on the aura, you will be guided when to stop. If you feel heat then you keep your hands there until the temperature returns to normal. The same applies to a feeling of cold or tingling. When all feeling returns to normal, you know enough has been given.

Usually the hands are kept still over the location of the problem area/s and will be moved only when guided to the surrounding areas. If, for example, a shoulder is to be treated, the hand/s will be placed over where you feel the sensation is the greatest. Once this area starts to feel more normal you might then feel the need to go to another part of that same shoulder to give healing there also. Often the pain is greatest where the actual wound, damage or illness is centred, but you will be aware that is spreads outwards to the surrounding area or tissue. This is why those areas also need to receive healing but not so much as the core area.

As we stated earlier another way of feeling a problem is by a feeling of magnetism in your hands. It is like a strong pull towards that area. This will usually mean that you need to work a slightly different way than keeping the hands still over the area affected. As you place your hands in the aura over the affected spot, you might feel a need to pull your hands backwards as though you are pulling something away from their body. As you do this, you will feel a pulling sensation, which will stop when you are far enough away. This will probably happen two to three times, maybe a little more, before you then feel a need to shake it out. This means you will feel a need to shake your hands as though shaking something off or out of them. You might even want to rub them on a part of your body to rub away whatever is there.

It is possible that you will probably repeat this procedure several times before feeling the sensation leave you. As soon as the feeling of a magnetic pull has gone, you know you have done enough. After this type of healing session, you will probably find yourself wringing your hands as though washing them. This is a natural way of cleansing yourself. There are those who say to wash with water after all healing sessions but this is not necessary. Go with what you feel to be right for you because as with all work you do with the spirit, you will be guided at all times. You might automatically want to do the cleansing of the hands after each healing session but you will always be guided when it does and doesn't need to be done. If you choose to use water then that is your choice but most true healers will feel no need for this as they place their trust in our guidance. We have heard said that a healer must wash their hands in water between each patient or they will transfer things from one person to another. This again is nonsense and a man made belief. By not washing your hands between each patient it is impossible to pass things from one person to another.

We have talked of the main ways there are for helping aid us in our healing work and how you may be able to find the problem areas that need to be worked on. The exceptions to this are illnesses such as diabetes, cancers of the bones or bloods and any of the many other illnesses or diseases that can affect the whole body. In cases such as these it is not possible to run the hands over the aura and pinpoint one particular area which needs help. If you are a natural healer, and we hope you are if you are doing this work, then you will usually be guided that an overall healing session is required.

You will often see a colour surrounding the person which will tell you that it is more serious or you will receive a "knowing". There are many ways of being able to tell what ails a person and even if you are not aware of the exact problem, you will know that the whole body has to be helped. The way in which you receive this information will depend on the other gifts you have and use. As we have said, all mediums have their own way of working and not all will have all of the supernatural gifts. Some will only have one whilst others will have varying amounts between one and the maximum allowed. It matters not how many of the gifts you have been given, nor does it say anything about how good or bad a person you are. What matters is how you use those gifts to help others.

At times, you will be told by the patient about which illness it is they suffer from. These are the people who often have the most hope, faith and belief that you will be able to help them. They do not need to play games with you and test you. It is a very great and wondrous thing that you are doing by assisting us with these people and we hope that those who work with us will always do so with humility and love.

As you will be aware not all people can be cured as everyone has their time to join us in the world of spirit. This does not mean that healing is never given though. For those who cannot be cured they shall always be helped in another way. As we have earlier stated, sometimes it will be to relieve some of their pain and suffering and at other times it could be to help them mentally in coming to terms with what is to follow.

Healing is not just for those who have physical illness but is also for those who suffer mentally or with stress. It is something which can be given freely to each and every human being if they so desire it. It is always a good thing for the families of those who suffer to also receive healing as they try to cope with their loved one's problems whatever they may be. This has often been done with great success for those who partake of the offer when given to them.

There are times during a healing session that we shall draw closer to you, the healer and the patient. You will know when we are there assisting you as you do when practising your other mediumship. It is not too often that we draw that close, but there are times when we shall let you know that we are with you and assisting in your work. It is not at all times this is needed. You have been given the gift of healing as an instrument of God and are able to do this yourself.

When we draw close, you will be aware of that chill which accompanies us. The reason we draw near at times is if the help of a specialist is required. Maybe someone who was a surgeon when of your world and who specialised in a problem area will want to come and assist you in giving healing. We do not do this very often in normal healing sessions but only from time to time. There are some healers though who we shall work with continuously on a day to day basis. There may be a team of specialists and surgeons from the world of spirit working tirelessly with a few chosen healers doing more specialised work. This is rare and only a few of your world are chosen for this work with us. The majority of you will be mediums who also have a healing gift, but for those who are to be these specialised healers working with us daily, this will be their only work.

We hope this section has helped guide you all a little into the ways of healing and some of what it entails. We know that there are many who will argue with you if you tell them that healing cannot be taught and you will usually find that those are the people who quite often wish to profit from it by charging large sums for their ministrations. We plead with those of you who wish to do this work with us in the correct way and who wish to work only with higher energies not to fall into this category. Costs have to be covered but not in a way to gain profit. Remember, God freely gives healing and we are used only to assist Him in the way He wishes. It is not a man made gift and as such it cannot be made up of man made laws. What God gives He can take away again so please use this most precious of gifts in the way it is meant to be used and do not abuse it. Remember, we reap what we sow.

CHAPTER NINE

Mediums and the way they work
A brief explanation about mediums

There are many ways in which a medium can work with us, and here we hope to explain briefly, what they are. There is mediumship, clairvoyance and psychic work. All of these at times are used by a true medium. There are far too many people today who think that clairvoyance and mediumship are exactly the same. This is not necessarily the case. Clairvoyance is when one sees past, present and future events and is not always given by those in the world of spirit. Mediumship on the other hand, is strictly working with spirit and is mainly used for giving evidence of those who have been before.

Mediumship gives information mainly about past events, people and places, some present and very little future. This is not done for those who want to have their 'fortune' told. It is done for those who have lost someone close to them at some time and wish to try to hear that all is well. It is for people who want to believe in a world beyond the one you all inhabit now. They are looking for proof of this. It is done in order to bring comfort to those who mourn, but information is not always given by the ones they want to hear from.

Clairvoyance is what most think of as fortune telling. Going for a quick reading to tell you some of what your future holds. This is mainly done psychically and uses the energy of the person sitting for the reading. It uses many of the psychic's senses, which have been highly developed over a period of time. It is this that most people could learn to do and that is why the mistakes have been made over the years by many who confuse it with mediumship and believe this too can be learned.

Many mediums and teachers today say mediumship and clairvoyance are part of the same thing. We tell you now that they are not. Clairvoyance can be a part of mediumship, but not the other way around. Being a clairvoyant does not make you a medium. That is an entirely different thing. People talk of too many fancy words today. Clairsentience, Clair hearing, Clair knowing and Clair seeing, Clair this and that. This is all completely wrong. We are now to teach you that this is not the case at all.

Many mediums have the ability to hear spirit, see, smell, taste and feel. They will usually have all of the same senses that one would normally have in your world. The difference is that whichever of these they receive whilst acting as a medium is not their own but that of another. Those senses given to you for yourself in life have no fancy names so why do you feel the need to give them when they are of spirit? We are aware that a few of these names are to enable those of you to be aware they come from us and not from yourselves, however, there are now too many names being used and it is not necessary.

Clairaudience - hearing spirit, Clairvoyance – seeing as we have already described, and Clairsentience – feeling, are the only ones needed to be used. All of the others they use today fit under one of those headings. There is no need for more. If you hear too many silly words being used, then that again should tell you that these are the people who like to be seen to be 'different' Not all of it is their fault as it can be that some teachers have taught them this way.

We have already stated that a clairvoyant need not be a medium and very often they aren't. It is therefore, very misleading to give names to all of the things a medium senses. If you insist on doing it then so be it, but just be aware that it is not necessary and it doesn't make you a medium just because you can name all of these things. The names are usually used to show off and to make you look and sound different from others.

A psychic will use a sixth sense, which everyone has the ability to do. It is something that all have within them, but due to lifestyle changes, has not been used for many eons now. There are those who have chosen, and will choose, to develop it and that is good. It is not good though that many have developed it only in order to become "fortune-tellers" thereby enabling them to charge large sums of money. Reasonable amounts are fine, but sadly too many charge far more. These are the people who can mislead others and can cause much upset. They will often throw in an odd "your grandmother says to say hello to you". There may be another comment similar, which can fit anyone or anything. This is **not** mediumship. It is pretence. Please do not go to these people and more to the point; please do not **be** one of these people.

That said, there are some clairvoyants working today who do so in innocence and purity of heart. They are offering a service, which many of your world wish for. The reputable ones will not charge large amounts of money and will not pretend to be mediums if they aren't. They are honest about what they do and admit to being psychics only. They will tell you that you must not change your life to fit with what they see. Nothing in life is written in stone. Things can change all of the time. What a clairvoyant sees may be right for that moment, but things can change to alter that path for many reasons. You have free will and must exercise that right at all times. It is not really how things are meant to be, but we understand that this will always happen and have no problem with those who act in a responsible manner.

If Clairvoyance is practised by a medium who uses it together with their other gifts, then it is usually done in a more responsible way. Sadly, this is not always the case though and these people can often be confused with the reputable mediums who have not been tempted by greed or glamour. As you can see from what we tell you here, vigilance is needed at all times. It is not all as simple as you thought it to be is it?

It is because this psychic ability can be developed by anyone at all that others think mediumship and healing can be also. This is completely false and is something that needs to be rectified as a matter of urgency. This is what we talked about earlier when we spoke of the standards of mediumship and who is being allowed in development classes. Please remember what we are telling you. A clairvoyant is not always a medium, but a medium will usually be clairvoyant. If you work using only psychic energy then you should call yourself a psychic or clairvoyant. If you work with spirit you should call yourself a medium.

It matters not that you might also work with psychic energy, if you are working with spirit and psychic energy you are a medium. If people stuck to these simple rules it would stop the confusion that exists. Sadly, practically everyone today of your world thinks that all can be called one or the other no matter what work they do. This is not so. We have explained the differences to you and would be delighted if you were to start changing the way things are now.

Nobody has the right to claim that their way is the right way. All who practice mediumship, in whatever way they choose, will probably have found a way that is right for them. None of you has to belong to any given church or group and need no certificates of authenticity or likewise credentials. Most of this paperwork means nothing. There are so many people today holding those very same pieces of paper who actually have no right to. They are not people who work with us in the correct way. We are the teachers, we decide who should and shouldn't work with us and we decide who is to work in whichever way suits them best. It is not for anyone of your world to do this. All you are able to do is help them with their development.

Those of you who practice mediumship properly may have a variety of ways of working together with us. Others may have one, some one or two and others will have all of the gifts. None of these ways is done identically to another. If you are someone who hears spirit then you will hear in a totally different way maybe to another. This cannot, therefore, be taught by anyone to be done in one particular way. The best teachers are the ones who are aware of this and work with their pupils accordingly. We shall now talk of some of the ways you may be chosen to work with us.

It is very important to state that not all of you will experience all of these things we are about to talk of. If you are at the very start of your spiritual path, you might only have one of these gifts whilst more advanced souls may have several. There are those who are very advanced indeed, who may well have all of the gifts. Do not be jealous or envious of another's gifts. Be happy with the one or one's you have been given. In time, all will be yours but this may not be the right time or even lifetime for that. You will also find that if you have several of these gifts that they swap and change through the years. The way you practice each of them may even vary from time to time. It is you who shall probably end up as the best teachers at some time and will be able to teach each new pupil individually or in small group rather than as is done today.

There are many ways in which we can communicate to or with you. The first of these that we talk of is by the way of hearing.

CHAPTER TEN

Hearing

The different ways in which this can happen

The ways of hearing are varied. Some will hear with an outer voice which appears as though someone is standing next to them and others will hear within their heads. It is not defined which of these is the better way as each person has to do what is right for them. We shall strive to communicate with you by whatever means we can but it is up to the individual person how that can be achieved. Some are more highly developed than others, which will enable communication to be done in a more simple way whilst others will be at the start of their awareness and development which makes things slightly harder for us all.

It matters not which way you are to receive this voice from us. As long as we are able to reach you that is the important thing. Not all times will it be just one of us talking to you. Sometimes, there will be more than one who wishes to communicate a message and this can then be more difficult. It is up to you I'm afraid to handle this as well as you can.

We in the world of spirit get quite excited when one of you starts to communicate with us and we sometimes get over excited. It is the same as yourselves. Our personalities come with us when we pass from your world and we need to learn to control this at times just as you do. Not all who communicate with you will be this undisciplined, as many will have been of our world for some time indeed. Others, however, shall be very young souls in the world of spirit and they have to learn some self-control just as your developing natural mediums sometimes have to.

These young souls in the world of spirit are never alone when they communicate with you. They will at all times be accompanied by an older more sensible soul who will help try and guide their endeavours to communicate. So you see, we too have teachers in our world, just as you do in the world in which you live. Patience must be extended at all times from each of us who do this work. The work of spirit that we have agreed to do is not easy for anyone. It is just as difficult for us as it is for you. The reason for this is because we have to change our vibrations in order to communicate with each other. We are of different worlds and on different wavelengths. In order to hear each other, we of both worlds need to learn how to adjust this when necessary.

The first time you hear us could be in a variety of ways. If it is within your head, you will be unsure at first from where it comes. It will be as a thought pattern going over and over in your mind that will not go away. It is not always clear and sometimes comes in a more muddled way. You shall then have to strive to grasp what it is that you are receiving. You will probably be very unsure where this has come from, what it is about, but as time goes on you will become more familiar with it, and we shall get better at working together. It shall become clearer and clearer and you will eventually be able to realise what it is that comes to you much quicker than you do when first experiencing it. It is not like knowing. This is a different sensation and it is only when you experience it you shall know what we talk of.

Voices, which are heard outside your head, are a different matter. These can be very muffled or very clear. Again, this will depend on the experience or ability of both the medium and the communicator. It can be one voice or several voices. When first hearing a voice or voices you may be unsure from where they come. It may seem as though there are people talking in another room nearby or even outside. If you are alone at the time, this can be very confusing for you. Do not worry if you cannot hear what is being said clearly at this stage, as it is not important.

Like all things in life, it takes time to learn. So it is with the gifts of the spirit that you have been given. They do not automatically appear overnight honed and polished. As a child, you had to learn to understand your family, their friends, and what it was they said to you. It took time until you understood it all. Day by day, you would learn a little more until one day it all came together. You were not even aware of when this day was; it just all fell into place. The same can be said with your speech. You had to learn to speak over a period of years. Hesitantly at first with one word here and there being spoken until eventually whole sentences could be formed

This then, is exactly what it is like with your spiritual gifts. A gradual awakening and plenty of practice until each one is perfected. It might not be that you will ever hear clearly. It may be that the voices you hear will remain slightly muffled and difficult to hear. At other times, the voice or voices may be very clear as though someone stands right next to you.

One thing we must be most insistent on is what you say to others. There are many times we hear what some mediums say to the ones who come to them and we despair. They add their own words to what we tell them. This should never be done. We cannot stress enough to you that you should only ever relate to others what you have been told and no more. If we have not said it to you then you should not say it to them.

There are those who teach that you should tell the one who has come to you things you have not been given. Never should this be done. If we want them to know something then we shall tell them. If it is not said then you too should not say it. They argue that this is acceptable as the person who sits with you wants to hear words of comfort or love and that it is only right you should give that to them. This is not correct. If the one who communicates wishes to gives those words of comfort or words of love then they would do so.

There may be times when the person concerned who has passed might not have been a demonstrative person in life in your world so why should they change that now? The one who wishes to hear from them would know that and would, therefore, not expect to hear it said. If you automatically say it each time you read for someone then you are not doing your work correctly. Instead of giving evidence, you would be doing the opposite as you are talking as the person communicating never would. That would not then convince the one who wished to hear from them.

There may also be times when the one coming through might not have liked the person they wish to communicate with. It could be that they have come through for an entirely different reason and if you gave your usual talk of love and comfort, it would be completely wrong. These are but a couple of reasons for not giving standardised messages. It is not for you to decide what is said but the communicator. You are but the mediator hence you are called a medium. This false evidence is one of the ways being done today that causes us great upset. It is an example of the shoddy mediumship that we do not agree with that is being practised in many places and that we would like to see stopped.

Those of you learning today, we beseech you not to adopt these ways. Please only ever pass on exactly what you are given. Do not add any extra words or nuances. It is not for you to do that. If you are meant to get more to follow then you will. Wait and see if more follows. If it doesn't then so be it. It might make no sense to you or the one who sits with you, but it must still be done that way. After returning home the one who has had the reading, may often later realise the meaning of something said, that was not apparent at the time of the sitting. If you had added those extra standard bits as taught you during your learning period by bad teachers, then that meaning would have been lost and an opportunity for good communication wasted.

Another thing that people of your world are doing today, is trying to interpret the message they are given. They try to put a meaning to what they are getting. This should not be done unless you are given a 'knowing' at the same time. If you see a knife or hear the word said, then say that. No more no less. If you see or hear the word garage, then say that. It matters not whether you know what these words mean. There are many people calling themselves mediums who will try to give a meaning for the things they say to you. They will talk of symbols and the meanings of these symbols. Anything we say to you is as it should be said. If the person you read for does not understand that when you pass it on, then leave it for now and go on to the next bit of the message. It might well be that as the message develops so the meaning will become clear.

Many mediums, both natural and forced, are tempted to say more and do so. If you don't understand something they have said to you they will say that in that case, it must be symbolic and they will try to make it fit with something you can accept. This is not true mediumship. This is what people do who are not communicating with us at all or who are just not good mediums. They are deluding themselves and the one for whom they sit.

Sometimes the genuine mediums are doing it because they feel they are not giving you enough information. The fact you have paid for a sitting with them, makes them feel they should be giving you more than they are receiving. The ones who do this are usually the ones who are very new to practising their mediumship and passing messages. They are still lacking confidence and faith in their ability to receive properly and think they could have missed something we have tried to tell them. They will learn quickly that this isn't the way they should be working

The ones who talk of symbols all the time and try to make things fit with what they have told you are the ones we are concerned over. Walk away from them and do not pay them large sums of money. If we wish to convey a message we shall do so. We have no need to talk in riddles or symbols. Likewise, if you see dramatic behaviour of any sort, for example with hands being cupped over ears asking us to repeat things, it is all for drama and effect and they are probably hearing nothing at all.

Any voice or voices heard are unique to you and no one else can hear them. It may be that one person will come through regularly to you and will act as your helper in all things spiritual of this manner. At other times, this may change to one you know nothing of. A name could be given to you of who it is that works with you, but this is not necessary for you both to work together well. Some say they are given a name when this has not been so. Some wish to give a name themselves to their helpers as it makes them feel more secure in their working relationship. We do not understand why this is needed as our work together will not be compromised by having no title.

There could well be times when names are given but this is by no means always the case. Do not worry over this as it will not hinder our work together. Some feel this in fact, can get in the way. There are those who become more intrigued with who we once were whilst of your world and what we did. This can then interfere with the work that needs to be done. This is a reason why so many times we do not give a name. If you choose to name us yourselves then so be it, but it means nothing. Where we are now we have no need for names; that is something that those of your world feel a need for and for us it is not necessary.

There are also some mediums who believe they have to give fancy names to those who they say work through them. These are often said to be of an exotic appearance or personality and most usually are said to be Chinese sages or Indian chiefs. Why they feel a need to do this we have no idea, but believe it is to make themselves appear more important and knowledgeable. There is an odd occasion when we do have these people communicate with our mediums, but it is by no means as common place as they would have you believe.

Then there are others who say they are communicating with those who were famous when of your world. Again, this is most often not the case as there is no need for them to be there unless the medium is reading for a member of that person's family or a close friend. Once of the spirit world we have no need to come back and talk to anyone unless it is for a purpose. We do not come and speak just to say hello. What is the point in this behaviour? The spirit world has no need of that, we only communicate when there is a real purpose and for no other reason.

In time, you will become familiar with those who work with you regularly and will recognise them without the need to call them anything. This is just another of the ways taught today for which we see no need. Being taught to reach one's guide and who that guide is, is a completely unnecessary exercise. You will come to know us and we will come to know you when the time is right. If you have to strive for this then the time is not right and you may end up reaching lower energies rather than those you really should be working with. This should be left alone.

We hope that this small section has helped you a little and enabled you to realise that not all who work with us hear or work the same way as each other. Some will hear voices clearly as though the person is still of your world. Some a muffled voice or voices which they have to strain to understand and others will have a mixture of the two. Then there are those who will never hear a voice per se, but will 'hear' in their heads. At different times, any of these ways can be used. It depends on the experience of all concerned; those of your world and those of ours.

Sometimes whilst giving a reading to someone, a medium may have several spirit souls all at once wanting to pass on a message to you. There can be one person or there can be coach loads! This will take tremendous discipline on the part of the medium. He/she will need to push the other voices back and try to listen to each in turn. No easy task for them to be able to do. This will become easier the more experienced they become.

As we have already said, each way is unique to you. Do not be put off by anyone else. Most especially, do not be fooled into thinking that this has to be done only one way. It doesn't. If you are comfortable with the way you work and all results are for good then that is what matters. Teachers of your world may guide you, but they must never, put words in your mouth, which is what many today try to do. Do not allow this to be done and do not allow them to tell you that the way you work with us is wrong. If we can communicate well and give accurate messages, then it is the right way, however that way may be. Stand firm. It is only by doing the things that we teach you that will enable us all to raise the standards of mediumship as we try to do with this book. The next we speak of is knowing.

CHAPTER ELEVEN

Knowing

Something all of you can experience without being a medium

Mediums who have this ability will be aware that they have it, as it is not something of which they can remain unaware for too long. It is quite a difficult thing to have at times and this is in itself quite a complex issue to be able to explain to anyone because it is not just a knowing of those things that are of spirit, but is also about that of your world. There are many things that will happen through your lifetime that you will have knowledge about and you do not know why or how you know these things. You just do.

Upon meeting people for the first time, one could take an instant like or dislike to someone they meet. Most people this happens to are not sure why it is. They cannot see any reason for their dislike of someone without knowing them and often find this disturbing. It makes them feel judgemental and so they try to overcome it and ignore what their senses are telling them. If, however, there is an instant liking of a person, they accept that without question. Mediums on the other hand, know exactly why they are feeling these things and will have learnt to trust what they are sensing. Even if the reasons may not be clear at the time, they just know and in time to come, no matter how long it might take, they will always be proved correct.

Another way of knowing is whilst doing a reading for someone. Unlike some of the other mediumistic ways this can be done, there are some things that you 'just know'. You have not seen pictures or visions of what you are telling them, you have not heard anything you just know that what you are saying is right. When you have this feeling, if it is of spirit there will be no doubt at all in your mind that what you say is correct. You will be one hundred percent positive that what you have just said is right. It is this positive feeling that shows you that you are working with spirit and that what you have said is not of your own mind. If you have any doubt at all about anything you say then it is probably not from spirit but yourself.

It is really quite impossible to explain this further to you as most would not understand it if they have not experienced it. We will often give this 'knowing' to you at a time it can help you most. If you are giving a healing session to someone, there are times you just 'know' that the person has been helped. Other times, you will know that they cannot be helped physically, but that the only help they are able to receive will be mental. This can be beneficial to you in your work as it will help you to deal with some situations that can be quite sensitive in nature.

Those who have experienced this will know what we mean. Knowing is also something that can be felt psychically. For example, was there ever a time you didn't want to leave someone as you felt something bad was going to happen. You try to shake off the feeling and leave anyway only to keep being uncomfortable and unable to shake off the sense that you know something bad is going to happen. Later you find out it did. You were right to feel that worry. This is something that everyone can experience. You do not have to be a medium to have this happen to you. This is part of your sixth sense being used as we talked of much earlier. We use this here as an example to help those of you who are not mediums understand a little better what knowing for a medium is like.

Other times it can be a knowing that something good is about to occur either to yourself or someone you know. That too can be correct. It is not just those scenarios though, but others also. The examples above just simplify it and show everyone that they can, or have experienced, that sort of thing themselves. They may well have done, but it will not be in the same way as those who have a proper sense of knowing. They will have been using their sixth sense whereas a medium is being given the knowledge from us. We have used these examples in order that everyone may understand better the work that mediums are doing. Any of you who are still developing your gifts will come to realise over the years that your 'knowing' gives you an insight that others do not have in many other ways.

It can be very difficult for someone in the early stages of developing and using their gifts, because they are not always aware that some thoughts they express are due to knowledge they have been given that others have not. You can be in a conversation with people about a subject you have never had experience of and yet find you know much about it. This sort of thing can happen often. It is not always recognisable as being as one of the gifts of the spirit.

It can make you appear to be a 'know all' and so you have to be very careful what you say. It is sometimes good to think before you speak. This is difficult for all of you whilst you are developing your gifts as there is much confusion to start with. There is so much going on in your mind that it will be very hard at times to distinguish what is real and what isn't. You are not a 'know all' as they think of it, but you do possess a lot of knowledge about subjects you may never even have studied. It is the same with your feelings, smells and all manner of spiritual gifts. You have to learn which are of spirit and which are of your world.

When you experience a knowing, people will not be able to sway you in what you say about these things. They will not be able to prove you wrong either. It matters not how long it takes to prove, but you will never be proved wrong. Every time you say you know something for a fact that will be the case. It really is a very good idea to keep most of this to yourself, as it will probably make you very unpopular. It will take quite some time until you are aware of this, as you will not know that this gift is from the world of spirit. You will yourself be bewildered at times by how you seem to know so much about certain things.

Do not worry unduly over this little matter, as time will help you to learn and discern what should and should not be relayed to another. There will be little problems along the way, as you will invariably upset some people by what you say whilst you are learning. These mistakes will never be bad or upsetting ones, just little blips. It matters not, as those who take offence are usually those with whom you will only have but a passing acquaintance. We all have to learn and as in any learning mistakes will be rectified as knowledge grows.

This gift then is really one for you to have for yourself. It is not really one of the gifts to be used for sharing with others. It is not a gift that will be used much when giving readings to people except in the instances already told you. The only time that will be the case, is when you have given information, which they do not accept. You will **know** that what you say is correct and will not be swayed. If you feel with utter conviction that what you have said is right then trust that feeling. The world of spirit is never wrong and will never mislead you.

The only times people are misled, is when those who are not natural mediums are trying to develop these gifts. They will achieve very minimal results and will be working with much lower energies and spirits who are out to deceive. These spirits will allow a few small results which are correct in order to flatter you and deceive you. The information you receive from them will be mixed in with a lot of untruths. It is the small successes they have that draw unscrupulous people into this field in order to mislead those who are in need of comfort. Sadly, the untruths will also be told to them and this is where the problems arise.

At this point we must reiterate that not all who wish to develop these gifts are bad people. In fact, far from it in many cases. Their only wish is to help and serve. The problem is with those who tell them they can do it and allow this very low standard of mediumship to be practised. They are deceiving the poor souls who believe themselves to be doing good. They have probably charged a lot of money for courses and classes which are nothing short of deception. Some of these teachers are themselves the product of bad or unscrupulous teachers before them so do not judge all teachers and pupils harshly. Remember in Christ's own words, "forgive them for they know not what they do".

When starting to develop your natural gifts, this is something you need to be very careful about. Only go to teachers who you know to be honest and truthful. You probably wonder how you will be able to tell. This is easy. By their fruits you shall know them. If they are full of ego and speak boastfully of how good they are in a loud immodest way, steer well clear. If they charge too much for a reading or healing, again they are not doing this work for the correct reasons. If they charge large amounts for teaching, then they are definitely not working in a way we would condone or accept as right and proper.

You will also hear tales of flying through the air and zooming through space. All manner of strange things will be told to you as will tales of mythical creatures. These people are not the ones with whom we work. Maybe they are doing these strange things they talk of, or believe themselves to be, but to what purpose? True spirit work is never done in this way regardless of what you might be told. If those strange ways are for you, then this teaching manual is not.

There really isn't more we can say on this matter as 'knowing' is not something that is generally used in mediumship when working, but is just another added extra so to speak. It is something given to you to help with what you do and not for the intentions of communication. It is this gift that allows you to discern the spirits and from whence they come. It helps you within your life and can also be used as an extra aid in passing information as a medium. It can help you to know when you have relayed the correct information. Trust is the key word when using this sense. Trust at all times. We will never let you down. Another complex sense or gift is that of 'feeling' and this is what we talk of to you next.

CHAPTER TWELVE

Feeling or Clairsentience

Mainly experience by mediums but also by everyone of your world in a small way

This is quite a subject to cover and we shall talk a little of the different ways in which one can feel. The first of these things are the most obvious. When reading for someone you may take on the feelings of the one who has passed. For example, if they died of a stroke, you might feel the same symptoms that they did. It could be numbness in an arm or a tingling sensation. The face could suddenly feel lopsided or any other manner of things they might have experienced. You may also find that your speech becomes slurred as you struggle to talk. As you are passing on the details to the one receiving the reading, you might find that you are having difficulty pronouncing some words correctly or even managing to say them at all.

Asthma attacks will often result in you feeling very breathless and struggling to breathe let alone speak. This feeling could also come with a possible tightness around the chest. Heart attacks will mean not only a pain in the chest but also the arm or face could feel strange. This is just a small example of what you could feel at any time during a reading. It is all quite normal and if you have asked to be shown how a person died in order to relate that to the one you are reading for, so may you also ask for it to be taken away from you. You will find that when asking for anything to be taken away it shall be done almost immediately. For certain things that you have felt much stronger it might take slightly longer. Just sit quietly for a short while until this has completely gone and then you can continue as normal.

There are many things you might feel during a reading and it all depends on how the person died. It is not just their manner of death that you shall feel, you will also at times be given an illness, pain or something similar that they might also have had to suffer during their lifetime. It could be that they were disabled and you are being given evidence of this by feeling. - such as the sensation of having no arms or hands. Maybe your legs will feel strange as though they are not there. It could be one limb or more. This is possibly because they lost a limb or were just unable to use one for whatever reason.

Your hearing could suddenly be affected, as your ears appear to close up thereby stopping you hearing properly. Everything could sound muffled and indistinct, or you could momentarily become deaf in order to show you that the person was deaf and what it felt like for them. Your speech may alter in a way that the person you are reading for recognises. Possibly the one who has died is giving you a speech impediment such as a stammer or a lisp in order that their personality comes over in a way that can be easily recognised.

There are all manner of things and ways in which you can feel. It is not just the physical that you will experience though, it is also the mental. There may be a feeling of deep depression, which can be quite overwhelming. Sometimes it could be confusion due to dementia or other conditions similar; sadness, great joy, happiness, frustration. All of the emotions can be felt very strongly. These things can add up and when put together can form a picture of the personality of the person you are relaying details about.

Sometimes you yourself will feel great sadness at some of the things you feel. It will be difficult at times to shake off the feelings that you have had or experienced. We shall take away from you whatever you ask, but your very strong sensitivity as a medium is what will make the feelings sometimes linger with you a little longer. These things are what make you such a good medium. Being so sensitive makes you suitable for this work. It is also why so many mediums are sometimes referred to as sensitives.

It is not necessary in the book we write now, to talk too in depth about any of these feelings and how they may feel to each individual who experiences them. The only real reason for this book is to teach how mediumship and healing should be done and by whom. We explain various sections only in order that you are aware of the different ways you might work as you develop and for those who are not mediums to also understand what it is you feel and what happens when a real and a natural medium is doing a reading. We do not wish you to be fooled by anyone who tells you to expect those things that are not of us.

Never exaggerate what you feel. You must only ever state exactly what it is that you are feeling. No more and no less. There is no need to play act as many do. There are those who like to add some drama and relate what they are feeling with great moans and wails of distress. They cry in great gulps and anguish. Never do this. If you are behaving as a medium really should, you will only feel these emotions or pains in a way to understand what that person giving the message felt. You are not experiencing it literally, as they felt it. It is not to the same degree as it would be should you really be having this happen to you. There is, therefore, no need for drama and histrionics. No one who relates anything to another in this manner, or any way similar, is a genuine medium acting with the humility that they should but are being theatrical for the sake of drama and to put on a show.

If you are told in any of your classes to add anything to any of the experiences you get, ignore them. They are wrong. We cannot tell you often enough. Only what you get should be given. Each pain one experiences is different to another person. All mental anguish felt is experienced differently also. How can anyone generalise with these things? As each person in life will experience everything in their own unique way, it is impossible for teachers to teach generalisations on how messages or details should be relayed and yet there are many who do. They try to generalise what is received and how you should tell about the experiences you are receiving. How can they? They are not feeling what you are. They are not acting as the medium at the time you are being given this information.

They can, therefore, not tell you what to say. All they can do is listen to what you have received and how you relay it to those in your group. They can then advise how it could be better worded, or maybe what you shouldn't say to avoid upsetting anyone thereby causing undue distress. When learning to develop your mediumship skills, it is very easy to word things wrongly due to inexperience. When you receive something very sensitive you should take your time and be sure what you receive is correct. There is no need to hurry. There are teachers and classes where they will try to make you hurry. It is almost as though they think, the quicker you are, the more accurate, impressive and experienced you sound. The important thing is to get it right. We are in no hurry and the person waiting to receive news certainly won't be.

There are teachers who tell you that the important thing is to just keep talking. They say that by opening your mouth and letting anything come out that you will be given the words to say. This is not right. In some ways a little of what they say is correct, but you should not talk incessantly. If you do, how can you listen? How can you hear? You need to wait to see, hear, or feel. As in all conversations they are not, or shouldn't be, one sided.

If you are talking non-stop, then the chances are you are not relaying accurate messages from us in the world of spirit, but are adding your own bits in as well. We need you to sit quietly and listen to us. No matter which way we work together, we need your attention. We cannot have that if you don't stop talking. This incessant talking does not usually happen in one to one sittings but is more frequently done in large gatherings. This almost gives a sense of showmanship and this work we do together should not be done that way.

It is not about showmanship it is about being an accurate and sensitive medium. A true, natural medium who retains their humility will never act in this way. Even though you may eventually work with us very quickly indeed, it is only on rare occasions that this will happen. It cannot happen every time. There are times when care is needed to be taken and it isn't. Sadly, many very good, natural mediums are drawn into the world of greed, glamour and materialism that fame can bring to them. We will talk of this in the section about charging.

There are mediums who are able to work very quickly indeed so do not think we say **all** should never do it that way, but even those who are able to will still take time to listen occasionally. They have periods when the words come out full force, non stop very quickly indeed. From time to time though they will need to pause and take stock again. It is, therefore, never non-stop all through the demonstration or sitting. If it is, then you know that they are also working as showmen/women and that their ego has taken over in order to try to impress.

Many good, genuine mediums have sadly been taken over by their ego's somewhat and it ruins their work and ours. We hope that we are to be able to put this right by telling you about some of these pitfalls. Some we are aware of work very quickly indeed and have a degree of show about them due to their personalities. They are not the ones with whom we have a problem. The mediums we dislike are the people who obviously think that they are the ones doing all of the work. They think that without them this work would not be done.

We ask you please to try never to become as they are. Try to keep your humility. Only give what you get. Remember that you are but an instrument helping in this work and that the gifts can be taken away if misused. Some of those who we speak of have had this happen to them, but they carry on as though this were not the case. Sadly, many believe them and go to see them. We need this to stop. This is not the way we intended for our work to be done. The larger the audiences and groups the more it is for show of the medium rather than the work they do. They are not doing our work they are pandering to their own ego.

Although this is a section on feeling and the different ways things can be felt it is still a book about mediumship. We would not be doing our work if we did not use this opportunity to teach those of you learning now the right ways. As we have said, the purpose of this book is to teach where it is all going wrong today. We need to correct many of these important issues and the best way is within the different sections of this book.

We have talked to you of feelings in the course of reading for people. What we haven't mentioned is the 'feeling' you may get on other occasions. These are very different and again, liken themselves to ones sixth sense. A 'feeling' that something is going to happen – good or bad. The 'feeling' that news is imminent about a particular thing. There are many ways this can happen as you are well aware. This is not something that is only for mediums to experience. You too who read this may well have had this happen to you.

The way a medium will experience this though, can be very different at times. Although mainly it will be as you yourselves experience these feelings, there will be times that a medium is given them for a specific reason. They will know the difference between the two ways. It is not something that is readily able to be described, but that is where their gift of 'knowing' will also come into play. They will 'know' that the feeling they are getting is different and is from spirit. There is no more we need to tell you on this subject and will now go on to talk of 'seeing'

CHAPTER THIRTEEN

Seeing

The different ways of 'seeing'; the future and the seeing of spirit

As with all of the other gifts of mediumship there are different ways of seeing. It also has different meanings. There is the seeing of future events and there is the seeing of spirit. Let us first talk of the seeing of the future

This is something that has caused so many problems in your world today. It is due to the fact that there are some small glimpses allowed of what is in the future that the term 'fortune teller' has evolved. There are those who just wish to make money by claiming to do this for others and this is something we wish very dearly to see stopped. We are aware that there are many genuine mediums and clairvoyants working today who are trying to do this work in a sincere and honest way. As you are only too aware, this is not the case with the vast majority of people who claim to be working with us.

One of the biggest dangers of the practice of fortune telling when done in the wrong way, is that huge numbers of people in your world are relying on the unscrupulous clairvoyants to tell them how to run their lives. They will go far too often asking what lies in store for them. They will ask what it is they should do next with their lives. An honest clairvoyant or medium will never allow this to happen. Sadly, there are many more who will. They are more than happy to give readings each time in order to take more money off them. It also gives them a feeling of being rather important. Please, we beg of you, do not go to these people. Do not encourage these practices to continue. We tell you now; those who are trying to become very rich are not working for or with us. They are working for themselves.

Those who can see into some future events are not able to do this at all times whenever they choose to. They are given but glimpses and not always are these glimpses very clear at all. For instance, a medium can be given pictures in their mind of an event to happen. They can see maybe a plane that has crashed, but not where or when. They could see the whole scene acted out in front of them, but are usually unable to prevent it from happening as all of the details are withheld. It is only when the event is seen on the news or some other such way that they will recognise the whole scene playing out before them as the one they foretold would happen. This is because certain events in life have to take place as it is in the order of things. Some things in life are not to be prevented.

What is the purpose of such a vision you may ask and quite rightly. The reason is in order to allow others to see that the rest of the work those mediums do is correct and truthful. If they foretell of an event they have seen, bad or good, which then happens, it gives credence to all else they say or do. It is not just bad things that can be seen or disasters, but also good things can be foretold also. A much awaited and longed for child that seemed to be impossible and yet by a miracle it is foretold and happens. Again, it will not say when or be explicit in detail, but it is there to give hope when hope had all but gone. This can be said of many future events and these are only a couple of small examples for you.

The way these visions are seen can be like moving pictures. Almost like being shown on a television or a big screen. The person receiving these visions can watch it all unfold in front of them almost as though they were part of it. It is very clear, sharp, and very real. At other times it can be fragmented and cloudy as though they are looking through a net curtain or a wispy cloud. The more fragmented visions tend to be of the more personal kind rather than major events. There are no set ways of it all happening though and the ways can vary with each vision.

It is not set that one person sees one way and another person a different way altogether. No, each person can experience many different ways of seeing. These mediums can also be called 'seers' for very obvious reasons. Anyone who tells you that they see many things in the future for you are either deluding themselves or lying to you. We never impart too much knowledge to them about anyone's future or about future events. A lot of what they are shown of future events can be very cryptic indeed and it is only later that it will become clear what it is that they had seen.

When anyone sits with a medium or clairvoyant, they should be there for the purpose these gifts were intended only. The gifts are meant to be used to bring comfort, hope, joy and faith that there is more to this life of yours than you can all see. It is meant to make them leave after a sitting knowing that there is someone or something far greater than any of you can comprehend whilst on the earth on which you live. It is only once you have left that place in which you now dwell, that you shall be allowed to see more of these truths.

It is for these purposes that during a 'reading' a small part of future events will be allowed to be shown in order to bring about that hope as well as comfort. It is also to be used at other times when credibility in one's work is needed to be proven to others. There are very few occasions when more information is given in order to divert or stop a disaster from happening. I am sure that many of you reading this may have heard of some of these things. Most people have a story to tell about something they have seen, heard or read about with regard to this. It is done in order that you may query the here and now attitude that many of you have today. If it stops and makes even one person think, then it has served one of its many purposes.

The other way mediums can see is not of visions but of people who were once of your world. Some, not all mediums are able to see those of the world of spirit. Yet others are able to see other beings not once of your earth. There are those whose spirits have left the world in which you live and who are now with us which is where you too will one day be. Then there are others who were never of your world but were meant only to dwell in the world of spirit in order to guide and help others throughout their lives.

Each person who lives on your earth is appointed one of these very spirits to be with you from the moment you enter your world until the day you pass out of it again. They are there to help guide you and guard you from all evil or harm. Some of you will be aware of that guiding hand and may at times pay heed to it. There are many times that this guiding hand is completely ignored though.

How many of you can think of a time in your lives where you kept getting a nagging feeling that you should or shouldn't do something? A time you kept feeling that you shouldn't get on a train or in a car and yet ignored it only to have an accident or something similar. You could have taken notice of that nagging feeling, thereby avoiding said accident or whatever else it may have been. That was your spirit friend or guardian angel which was appointed to be with you. That nagging feeling is their way of trying to help guard and guide you through life.

You are probably thinking right this minute that they aren't doing a very good job then. Why aren't they making it much clearer in order for you to avoid these pitfalls of life? The answer is because you all have free will. We cannot interfere too much as you alone have to decide what happens to you in your life. It is your path and journey and we cannot dare change that course for you. That is why we can only give a guiding hand at times in order to maybe nudge you a little.

There is an odd occasion that we are allowed to intervene. It is when by a quirk of fate you are in the wrong place at the wrong time. You may be about to have a dreadful accident and lose your life which is not meant to happen. This is the only time we, or your guardians, are allowed to intervene. They are able to save you and change the course of things for you in that instance. You will recognise an event like this as something that happened that you cannot possibly explain no matter how hard you try. An inevitable accident that couldn't have been avoided and yet it was. Finding yourself on the other side of the road and not knowing how you got there only to see that the exact place where you had been standing a car had mounted the pavement or a cement block had fallen from a building right where you had stood.

If any mediums were standing nearby, they may have seen what it was that moved you and saved you. They could have seen your angel or guardian carrying you to a place of safety. Not all mediums can see this way, but some can. They can also see those who stand near you and who talk to them passing you messages. They will see not in their minds eye as we talked of before, but they can actually see them as a real, solid person.

Of course there isn't a solid person standing there, but they will be given this vision in order to help them in their work. There are other occasions where they can see things such as auras around people. The aura is your body energy which we talked of at the beginning. Some mediums can tell you the colours or the extent to which your aura extends from you. There are many things they can see, and some of it is as clear as though it were a solid object.

The things mentioned above are some of the occasions where a medium may be allowed to see into the future in order to help prevent something such as that occurring. You have heard tell, stories of people who saw something bad was going to happen and warned the person concerned. When heeded, they have helped prevent a tragedy that was not destined for them at that time in their lives. It could be that on some occasions there will be a vision of a greater tragedy that they are given knowledge of. It is not often that this will happen. It will be done in order for them to give warning to the people who will be involved. At these times, there are many who will laugh it off and say it is a load of nonsense. They are the ones whose time it most probably is to leave the world you inhabit. The ones who do take notice and alter their plans are the ones who were not ready to leave your world at that time.

We hope you can understand a little more now of how mediums are working by these descriptions. How some work in one or two of these ways, some only have one way of working and others who are very highly developed and evolved may have all of these gifts at their disposal at varying times. It is very difficult for those of you who do not experience these things to understand. We realise this, but hope the brief explanations we have given you will help a little. We now go on to talk to you of writing.

CHAPTER FOURTEEN

Writing – Automatic

This chapter explains what automatic writing is and how it is done. It also talks of automatic drawing.

There are two types of writing. One is inspired and the other is called automatic writing. For example, this book, which we write with the help of our instrument is what you would call inspired writing. There is another way of giving information though which is called automatic writing. Let us now try to explain the differences to you in order that you understand them a little better. Both types of writing are actually given by one other than yourself. First, we shall talk to you of Automatic Writing.

Automatic writing is when a person sits with a pad and a pen or pencil and waits to see what words are given to them. At times, with a medium who is not adept at this it will be an unintelligible scrawl and at the other end of the scale it can be completely legible and full of meaning. It might take some time to be able to achieve receiving automatic writing properly and will take discipline on the part of the one receiving it in order for it to be done properly and effectively.

The writings received in this field are usually from one or more of your helpers who are with you each time you work. They know you well and will work with you each time you practice your mediumship. They are there to help you in your quest to know more of your life and those connected to you. At times, they shall also give information to you about future events to do with the world or those in it.

Each medium in life has one or more people in the world of spirit who helps them in their spirit work. Some are with you constantly and others will come and go when needed. The ones who work with you in your automatic writing are those same spirits who work with you in your everyday mediumship. Those of you who receive automatic writing will always know what it is you are doing when partaking of it. Those being inspired do not always know at the time that this is being done.

There are times, it must be said, that when receiving automatic writing one's own higher self can intrude and take over from the words given from spirit. It is such an easy transition that it is not always possible to realise when this has occurred. It is very rare that this will happen when receiving anything inspirationally as it flows too easily. When one's own thoughts start to intrude properly, it is very obvious as hesitation will occur. That is a clear indication that spirit has moved away or your mind has wondered and you should stop what you are doing immediately.

Not all mediumship needs peace and quiet or lack of intrusive noise. Automatic writing does. It can be done with others present, but is usually done when the medium sits alone and quietly. Anything at all that can distract the sitter should be attended to before attempting this. Telephones are the worst distraction along with animals, children or doorbells. It is, therefore, best to choose a time to do this when all of those distractions are least likely to cause any interruption.

Automatic writing can be attempted at any time you feel you wish to try and connect with those of the world of spirit. You can ask questions or you can allow words just to be given to you. Find somewhere comfortable to sit and make sure you have enough paper and pens to hand.

As with the exercises we taught you at the beginning you will need to clear your mind and prepare yourself to start working with us. The more experienced and comfortable you become with this, the quicker and easier you shall find it. The one who writes with us now is able to start immediately she sits with us. It wasn't always that way so do not be disheartened if at first nothing happens.

It is usually better to have a lined book, refill pad or similar to do this well. On the first sheet of paper, you should write the day, date and year at the top of the page for future reference. When you feel calm and relaxed enough, then you can start. As with all work of this kind ask for your protection and that you only work with those who are from God. Say that you only want the truth and nothing else. You are then ready to begin.

Hold the pen or pencil on the page and do nothing. Just poise it ready as though you were about to write something yourself. At first nothing at all might happen. Give yourself about 10 minutes the first time you try this and if nothing has happened in that time, then stop and leave it until another day. Sometimes, it is possible that you need these few times just to get comfortable with the idea of doing it.

There may be movement of the pen at times that is so slight, you won't be sure if you imagined it or not. This is you and your helper adjusting to each other and both your energies. There will come a day when the pen will move a little more positively for a moment. It could just be a scribble of twirls and loops that are all joined in one long line, or it could be a line of numbers. The number eight is very easy for us to do and so this is rather a common one for those starting out to receive at first.

When it first happens do not be alarmed. It will possibly startle you. If that is the case don't worry. We too have to get used to working with you don't forget. Put the pen down and leave it until another time. It is very important that you do not sit for too long at these early exercises. In fact, you will find as you become very adept at working with us in this way, that we spend very little time when we give you messages received in this way.

Once you start to receive writing that you can read and understand, you will become more confident and will find that you are able to 'tune in' to us more quickly for future sessions. As this happens, it is advisable to write on every other line in the book as it will be able to be read far easier that way. We have to tell you at this point that the writing you receive will be nothing like your own. It may even be very old fashioned in your eyes and full of loops and swirls.

There will come a time when you are so comfortable working together that your hand will move at speed and you will be able to write far quicker than your normal way. You will also find many pages are filled with writing very quickly and your hand and arm will not ache or be affected at all. Although you are sometimes aware of what words may be coming next, never try to pre-empt them. If you do, your mind is likely to start interfering. Doing this will also stop the words from coming and you will have to start all over again. It is only when all the writing has stopped that you should read back what you have been given. You will probably be aware of some of it and other parts will surprise you.

The content of what you receive can vary greatly. There is often a mixture of what we tell you. Some could be about people in your life or situations. Then there could be a couple of future events given to you or maybe just some philosophical thoughts for you to ponder on or share with others. There is not a set way for this and each spirit helper works with their instruments in their own ways.

As you become more experienced at receiving this writing, and depending on the level of your mediumship, you could well have several different spirit guides/helpers come through with different messages for you in any one sitting. It could well be, that they are to work with you at some time in the future and just want to say hello to you. At these times, the writing will alter and be different from that of your usual helper.

You may not feel anyone with you whilst you are doing this work as it is not always necessary for us to let you know we are with you in that sense. It is enough to know that we are allowed to work with you and you with us. We thank any of you who allow us to do this. Not all of you will be able to achieve it as it may not be what you are intended for so do not be concerned if this is the case.

A truly gifted medium need not feel that there is spirit with them when working in this or any other way as it is not always necessary. The one important fact is that they be comfortable. If there is any sense of nervousness then stop. Of course at first you shall feel slightly apprehensive but that it totally different from feeling something isn't right. Trust your instincts at all times.

Those who are very gifted and experienced mediums will know when it is their usual guide/helper with them doing this. You will be able to sense their presence but in a quiet calm way. If more than one is to speak with you, there will be a difference in the style of writing. You will feel the pen move differently and will feel the pen being controlled in a different way. You will also be aware of a different personality having stepped forward as they take their place near to you. This can happen several times in one session. It is not likely to happen until you are very experienced at doing this though so do not worry when in the early stages of learning.

A true, natural medium will be aware of the many differences when working with us and in the various fields we shall work together. Those who work in a limited field might not though be aware of this fact. It is of no matter. A natural medium will be aware they work with us without the need to feel our presence at all times. They just know when they are working. This cannot be explained to those who do not work in this way.

It does not mean they will never feel us because they will. It is just not necessary at all times. There are many ways to work together. Some of which we have already explained. Not all of you will work in all of these fields but some may. Those who do will be aware how each can feel totally different from the other. Each spirit feels different as you feel their different personalities. Also, the ways of working will feel different to one another. Mediums too will have their own unique way of working as will the spirit they work with. Each has their own personality and character and those are used when working just as much as any other sense.

Another way of working is by automatic drawing. This is done the same way as the writing only this time the medium receives pictures instead of words. It is usually of animals or people. Most often, the drawings will be done during a reading when the photograph can show the person who has died and is passing a message. It is another way of giving evidence that what the medium speaks of is correct. There are not many mediums who work this way and some will only do it at demonstrations when another medium is speaking. They will sit quietly at the side and sketch away as the medium who is talking passes messages.

After each person has received a message, the one who has been drawing will then show the picture they have done. It is most often of an animal that belonged to the person or someone they knew. There are others who say that they are drawing spirit guides. These are usually Indians for some reason. We do not know why so many of your world believe that all who seek to help from our world are red Indians or Chinese sages. It matters not to us, but these latter pictures should not be taken too seriously by anyone as they are often only from the mind of the person doing the drawing and not as given by us in the world of spirit.

There is no need at this time to tell you more on this matter as you will now have enough information to allow you to try what we have said for yourselves. Please be very careful as with all works you undertake with the world of spirit, that you only work with those who mean well. If you are pure of heart and your intentions are good then there should be no problems. The problems arise with those who are not naturally gifted and who try to force these things to happen. If you are a natural medium, you won't need to be told how you can tell, you will just **know**.

As with all of the different forms of mediumship, automatic writing is no different. Beware those who tell you untruths. Anyone receiving writing that only ever tells of disasters to happen and nothing else or on the other end of the scale just about wondrous things that are to come to them must beware. These are probably not the spirit you should be working with. There will be times that future disasters might be told to you and there will be other times that good things can be said. These should be interspersed with other information though. By no means should either of these things be all you receive. If it is, then as before, stop. Do it no more as you are obviously not meant to do this work and are attracting the lower energies.

CHAPTER FIFTEEN

Inspired Writing
Mainly done through mediums but sometimes by other people

Inspired writing is different. It is given by those in spirit who may come to you only for this one purpose. Those who write this book do so only for one reason, to spread the words that we wish those in your world to hear. We do not work with this instrument in any other field of her work as she has other spirit helpers for that. We are however, aware of what it is that she shall do in the future. We are also aware of what has been achieved by her in the past and present which does not involve this work of writing with us. She has also received automatic writing and those who work with her on that are not the same as those who work with her now to write this book.

We work in different ways and this book of instruction is being done in order to reach many people so that our wishes will be made known as far afield as possible. Inspired writing is exactly what it says. It is meant to inspire not just those who receive it and who we use for this purpose, but also those who will read what we say and maybe act upon it. What words are given in inspired writings are usually for the benefit of many. Not just of your world but ours also. It is mainly given in order that we can teach you how we wish lives to be led and how our work together should be done.

There are many people of your world who have written masterpieces. Some were inspired writings, which are well read and received by many. It is not always known by the author, or those who have read these works, that they were inspired by the world of spirit. It is not just words but music also can be received and inspired by the spirit world; great artwork and paintings also. Music that moves people in such a way that it feels almost unworldly probably is just that. Poetry that makes one sit and think about the world and the ways of it can also have been inspired.

Inspired writing and other works are not always recognised as such. We use it on many occasions when we need to tell or show those of your world things they need to know of or think about. The ones we use for this purpose are not always aware that it is not they alone who have produced these things.

Many of those who you call the great masters have actually been instruments in this work and some were aware of this fact but could not say anything for fear of ridicule. Others again had no idea that those of us in the world of spirit were inspiring them. This is really the fundamental difference in inspired writing and automatic writing.

The other way in which we use this manner of communicating is in order to reach as many people as possible. There is much wrong in your world today and we have tried to reach a lot of people so that they can tell the world what it is we wish them to know. Many have refused to do this work for fear of ridicule or harm from others. It is not an easy task to undertake doing work for the spirit world. There are a lot of people who have turned their backs on us and for that reason we are truly grateful to the one who helps us now. It has not been easy for her to do this book and she too, has been ridiculed by many.

We are to ensure that these words we give are spread for all to read. We are aware that many people of your world will ignore what it is we have to say through these inspired writings, but for each who ignores us, there are many more who shall listen and take note.

Writing these books is one way we can teach people our ways to help them improve their lives in order that the world in which they live can also be saved. We now use several people to help us in this field of writing in order to reach far places that may otherwise not hear of our work. There are to be many works such as this undertaken until we feel there is no more we can do. It is not to be an easy task for any of us and the one we use now to write this book for us is to have much more to do with us in the future.

There is a lot we have to tell you and by inspiring mediums to take our words down and spread them to others means that changes can after all be seen before things get too much worse. There is so much that you don't understand, but in time, with more of these teachings from us, we hope you will become clearer on some points we shall make in the near future. There is so little time for this work to be done as there are not many who will agree to undertake this work with us. There are also many people today who do not wish to be told these things as they believe themselves to be of a higher knowledge then is rightfully theirs.

They cannot know the things we try to teach and they get things wrong so often because they refuse to listen to us. There are so few people today willing to help, but many more are now to follow. The way is being opened up for others to follow in this work that we have now started and they must be taught the correct ways first. We need them to listen to us and learn the right way to do things as they develop the gifts they have been given, in order that we may work well together in bringing about the changes that are to come. This book we have inspired our willing pupil to write with us is where it all begins.

We hope that these words will inspire not just our friend we work with to spread the word, but also you, in order that you might have listened to what has been said. We hope that you will have been inspired to start helping to bring about these changes that are needed by not accepting the bad teachings which we have discussed in these pages. You can help us by demanding higher standards of teaching and teachers. You can then in turn go forth and teach as we have taught you within this book.

Much more is to follow on after this my friends and soon now you will hear of these words of wisdom that we wish to impart to you all. For now though, there is enough here that will enable you all to start the work we wish to see being undertaken. We wait to see what changes you shall help us bring about. You, the ones who read this book of instruction are very important to us as you are the future of change. You are to be instrumental in inspiring others as we hope we have inspired you with these writings. We hope you will go now and help us in our work. Be assured, we shall be beside you at all times helping. All you need to do is ask. We cannot come unbidden. We can let you know we are there, but cannot start to work with you properly unless you allow us to.

There are other ways we can inspire you to do something we wish to be done. It is not just by words alone that one can be inspired to spread the word. Actions can speak far louder than any words and this is where some of you who are not mediums shall come into play for us. You might find yourself inspired to do something never before thought of or done. Be assured that when this happens we shall be there opening the doors and paving the way for you in order that your work shall be recognised. So you see, there is not just one way of inspiration working in your world, there are many. Inspired writing, painting, music and actions of all kinds that in turn inspire those who see or hear what it is that you do.

CHAPTER SIXTEEN

To charge or not to charge

When charge is acceptable, when it isn't and how much it should be

Charging for your services. This is always a subject matter that causes us great concern. It is of our opinion that charges should be kept to a minimum. Too many people today are treating this as a money making exercise and forgetting what the reason for doing this work is really all about. It is a sad fact that we need to remind you all about this and to advise you how it should be done correctly in order that no offence is given. We touched on this a little earlier, but now need to speak of it more fully.

Where charges are made for renting or hiring rooms or places for this work to be done, then obviously a charge should be made to cover those costs. That is not meant to say that you can ask whatever amount you like. Too many people are charging far too much money for this work and it is not for the right reasons. It is only a means for them to make money rather than to help us in our work. If a charge is to be made in order to meet one's living costs then this should also be kept to a respectable amount in order to facilitate this.

If the medium is not doing enough work to meet their living costs then that does not mean they should charge a lot more per reading. Instead, they should find alternative work and do their spiritual work at other times. We have never intended for our spiritual work to be used in this way. For those who become well known in the field of mediumship the same rules apply. Obviously, there could be times when travel and accommodation may become necessary and these costs will need to be covered. That does not mean that it is an excuse to charge much higher prices in order to greatly profit also. Sadly, there are many who do this.

There are times when sitting with someone to help them when you might feel it wrong to make a charge at all. This is far more pleasing to us. We would wish that it were possible for this work to always be done without charge. We are aware that in your world, this is not always possible as bills need to be paid and food bought. Obviously, money has to be earned in order for one to live a normal life. It is not, however, acceptable to overcharge at any time at all in order to make excess amounts to live a more lavish lifestyle. The basic requirements are all you should be covering with these charges.

Healing is a different matter. Never should a charge be made for healing. The only time this is ever acceptable is if you need to pay costs or charges for where the healing takes place. Then only the costs for this should be met. Donations only rather than a set charge are how it could be done. If there is anyone who is unable to donate then healing must always be given free of charge. You are not the healer you are but an instrument used in this process. Therefore, it is not for you to decide that a charge should be made. We are aware that some people find it hard to accept help without giving something in return, in these cases it is acceptable to receive a small token from them if they so choose but it has to be an amount of their choosing.

There is one far greater than you who is the Healer and you are but an instrument who has agreed to be used to assist in this process. There is a scale by which this work is done and you are but one in the order of things. Many are used to assist in this work and also the work of mediumship. Some were once of your world and many more are of the world of spirit. There is an order to all of this and it is not for you to question how it is done or who is chosen to help or be helped. Remember, what is given can just as easily be taken back. If the gifts you have are abused or misused in any way, then they can, and probably will be, taken from you.

The ones who tend to misuse these gifts the most are those who are not truly gifted at all. They are the ones who wish to misguide the impressionable, weak people who come to them by telling tales supposedly about the future. These are the very people most likely to charge the most money. They are preying on the weak and vulnerable. They are the ones who are giving pure clairvoyance, mediumship, and the real work of the spirit a bad name. They are nothing to do with us and we do not work with them. They work alone and much of what they do is of their own minds.

Again, we shall upset some people who read this and disagree with us. Why should they disagree? If they too choose to work in this way then they are not doing God's work or the work of spirit. They are fooling themselves and others. We wish for this way of working to be stopped. It should never be associated with the work of real mediums who work with humility and whose only wish is to serve well and as honestly as they can. If these charlatans wish to work in their own way and by their own rules, they must be honest and say that they are not working with us or for God. They are working for themselves and of themselves only.

We refer to God whilst we talk with you of this work and many of you will be surprised to hear this. If you wish to refer to Him by any other name of your teaching or belief then so be it, but we shall refer to Him our way in order to keep this as simple as possible without causing offence. The reason for this is the instrument we use for this book is a believer of this faith and we respect those beliefs as we respect all beliefs, which work for the greater good. It is very important that you all do remember though, that by no matter what name you choose to call it, there *is* someone or something far greater than you at work. This, you shall discover at the time of your passing from your world into ours.

We hope this has cleared up the matter of money for you. We realise it is always a very difficult thing for you to decide about when doing this work with us. Costs of travel must be met and any other expenses and we realise this. We do not wish any of those who work with us to have difficulties due to the work we do together. Please do as we ask though and keep those costs to a minimum in order that it is not abused. We thank you for this, as we are sure that everyone who has read this far into the book will be a true follower and will always work honestly. Those who are annoyed or upset by what we teach will probably have stopped reading this long ago in disgust because it shows them in a bad light. They are the ones who do not wish to acknowledge that what they do is wrong or that the way they behave is incorrect.

We know those of you who are to work with us in an honest way and we will always help whenever we are able to ensure your needs are met at all times. It will not always be in great degrees but will enable you to survive and live without worry in order that your work may continue. You have not been chosen to work with us only to find you cannot do it due to life's needs. Have faith at all times. Ask and you shall receive. Do not feel guilty about making a reasonable charge, as you are not expected to be out of pocket for doing this work.

There are going to be times when you shall come across some healers or mediums who have made much money in their lives or who appear to be leading a more privileged life than others. This does not indicate that they are doing things the wrong way. Not all who work for us shall make little money throughout their lives. There are some who are to receive greater amounts in other honest ways. This is for reasons that do not affect their work. There may be a reason to do with their life lesson that this is to be so. It is also due to the fact of the way they are working for us. Greater work deserves greater rewards. Besides, those who truly work for us will most probably use some of their greater wealth to help others.

There are many ways that a lot of money can be amassed whilst working for us and it is not always incorrect. The times this is wrong, is when the individual charges made for helping people is too high. For example, you may go to a hall or a theatre to see a medium or hear them speak. They have to pay for the hire and maybe their travel and lodgings. You will then have to pay for tickets to see them. However, it is the cost of these tickets that shall tell you if they are working more for the money or for us. If the cost is kept to a reasonable level then they are still true to the work they have been chosen for. If the price is deemed far too high, then maybe ego is taking over.

We ask you not to encourage those who ask for too much money. Again, as in the teachers, we ask that you too remain vigilant and help us to eradicate these practices. This can be done by not attending events that are too highly priced. Not paying for readings that are of an astronomical cost and for walking away from classes that charge too much or have poor teachers.

We leave the actual amounts to our mediums as each has their own needs. What is right for one is not necessarily right for another. Different lives, areas in which one lives, family responsibilities and many more things can come into play. There is no standard or set fee. For each one it will be different. You will know whether it is reasonable or not. We leave it to your discretion. For those who retain their humility and keep their charges to a sensible and acceptable level, their work will increase. For those who become greedy and full of ego, they shall see their work start to become less.

People such as those who charge high sums will always have clients who wish to come to see them as people are sadly fooled by the fact that the more one charges the better they must be. That is not the case so please do not be taken in by this. We have told you all we can on this matter and now it is for you to go and make up your own minds. Remember, each one of you has free will. Judge not, lest you be judged. If in doubt, just walk away. Never berate another as you do not know what their life path is or what the final outcome shall be. Just remember the lessons you have been taught, that is all we ask of you. The only person you are responsible for is yourself.

CHAPTER SEVENTEEN

Teachers and teaching
Where can people go to develop their natural gifts and who is to teach them

On starting out in their work a medium will most usually begin in their home or those of their friends. They will try to practice on them and see what happens, this usually then progresses to doing little house parties or similar. Others will go to various workshops or meetings they have heard of and others again will go to spiritualist churches. Some will have no idea where to go or what to do but most in the end, due to lack of anywhere else to go, will end up in a spiritualist church.

The sad fact is that there are very few places for a natural medium to go to in order to help develop their gifts. You may think we are incorrect in this statement due to all of the spiritualist churches and meetings that they and other spiritualists have for this very purpose. Well, not all mediums are spiritualists. In fact, most of the natural ones aren't.

Where do these people go then? They don't is the answer most of the time. Unfortunately, it is most of the spiritualist teachings today that are compromising the standards of mediumship that we talk of in this book.

There are a lot of very good people in spiritualist churches and of these many are very good natural mediums. There are also many more within them who are not natural mediums and should not be acting as such but who do. We do not decry these churches or people as they have been working very hard and doing their best to offer a service that is much needed.

So what do we do about this? Where are we going to teach our mediums of the future who are not spiritualists if that is all your world has to offer? A very good question. This is where we hope this book will help. We would like to see new doors being opened for the smaller groups that we have talked of in this book and for those developed mediums who agree with what we say to act as the teachers in them.

We need to see smaller groups where each new member is assessed to see if they should be allowed to do this work. It is by no means for everyone and we need to see the practice of accepting all people and putting them in development groups stopped. We wish to see some of the practices now undertaken at awareness groups abolished also. Today, there are too many places allowing just anyone to walk in the door and say they want to be a medium or to join awareness and development classes. These people are then accepted and placed in a group of like minded people and told to partake of exercises that they should never be doing.

Awareness classes are good for all people if done in the ways we have described in this book. They are suitable for everyone whether they are mediums or not. That said, there are a lot of very strange practices going on in most awareness classes today. Why are people titling tables and trying to move objects? What is the point of this childish behaviour? It is the work of lower energies that we have told you of and warned you about. Why are these people who profess to be experienced mediums doing this then? We wish to see classes where none of this silly behaviour is done. There is no need. It proves nothing at all even though they say it does.

If you are to be a medium you shall already have been selected and will most probably already be aware of this fact. There is no need to do these acts as you will know exactly when we are with you without circus performances. Sadly, a lot of people want these things as they think it makes it more exiting and thrilling. It can make their hearts race, put a little bit of fear or nervousness into them and cause gasps of awe. We never work in this way. Those are things done by the ones with whom we do not wish to work.

It is not their fault. As we have said before, many of these practices have been passed down through many years and the ones who teach it today, are themselves only teaching what they too have been told are correct methods. We have a hard struggle on our hands to stop this and it is going to take a long time. Many decades of this way of teaching cannot be undone in a day or even a few months, it will take a lot longer until we see the changes we so desire.

It can change though and you are the ones who are going to help us do it. We want to see the mediums who agree with us start the small groups we talk of. These groups are to be of no religious denomination in particular and are to be for people of all beliefs, unbelief's and faiths. They will just be called mediumship classes and will be run in an orderly and disciplined way whilst having fun. They are to be relaxed and happy without the need for frills and thrills.

Those of you who are not naturally gifted mediums but who would love to help us in our work can. You can help by allowing us to hold these classes in places you may have available for that use. Whether it is your home or any other place you have that might be suitable, it would be a way that you can help us in our work. You can provide and make tea and coffee maybe for afterwards and sit with them when the session is over and listen to what they have to say about what has just taken place that evening.

It is by setting up these smaller classes around the world, that our words will spread out and reach others. When the fruits of these new ways of teaching are seen then people will come to recognise the truth of our words. We implore you to work with us on this. Maybe talks can be held in halls, assemblies and at other general meetings to spread these things we now say to you. Reach out and try to spread our words in whatever way you can.

There is no more to say today on this subject as we shall follow up with a booklet on instructions for teachers at a later date, in order to let them know what it is we would like them to do for us and with us. That is not for this book. For now it is enough that you go and start this work for us by spreading the word and by leaving any groups you feel may be teaching the wrong ways.

CHAPTER EIGHTEEN

Where to work

Describes the various places we would like to see this work done

There are many ways in which a medium works, which in turn, means many different places and times for them to do it. There is no one set place for this work to be done and can, in fact, take place at any time. There are the obvious venues of halls, theatres, churches and of course one's home, but that is not where it ends.

A true medium who has been awarded these gifts naturally, will at times be called upon to pass a message when in the strangest places. It is not often that this will happen but it can and will. Most of the teachers today are saying that this should not be allowed to happen and that the mediums need to discipline themselves. This is incorrect. If you have been chosen to act as a medium then you can be called upon at any time there is a real need to pass a message. It is not often that it will happen in this way, but it can and does. To tell you that is undisciplined is completely wrong.

Undisciplined behaviour is when a medium is learning how to work and can often do it with the wrong people and in places where they are ridiculed. That is because what they are doing isn't wanted. They need to learn to curtail this practice and most of them soon shall. They quickly learn that it isn't right to do it anywhere and everywhere just when it suits them. We understand why some do this at the start. It is because they want to learn and develop their gifts more readily. They choose the wrong people to practice on and open themselves to ridicule. It matters not to us as it shows they are willing and eager to work with us. We liken it to a child who does everything they can to please their parent only goes about it in the wrong way.

They are like our children to us and this floundering about in the early stages makes us smile. They are some of the ones who will become our best mediums as they are allowing the world of spirit to teach them naturally. Like all children, they will soon come to realise that what they are doing is not actually helping them, but is in fact, doing quite the opposite. Do not let it worry you if you are one of these people. What we would ask though is that if you are still doing that, would you now please stop it. Thank you.

For those who are learning, it is best to keep within one's home or that of your friends to practice. Only do it when they are happy for you to and never at any other time. You can do the exercises that we have suggested at the beginning of the book. In time, we hope that there will be more places set up that you can learn to develop your gifts properly and in the way we would like to see it done.

For those who have developed and are now working with us, you are possibly working in a variety of places that we have already mentioned. The only reason we have this very brief section, is so that we can ask you where not to use these gifts for work. We do not like the use of huge theatres and stadiums as this is not the way our work should be done. The whole idea of mediumship, is for us to work together in order to pass messages to and bring comfort to those of your world. For us to do this properly, we need to see you work in smaller venues where more of the people there can receive some words of comfort.

By using huge stadiums and theatres, there is little chance of anyone getting a proper message. It can happen and it does, but it is by no means a satisfactory way of working for either of us. Those who choose to do this are the ones who have possibly been carried away with the glamour of it all through no fault of their own. Not all of these people are bad mediums practicing in the wrong way. They have possibly been carried away with the need from so many people to see them at work. The very gifted mediums are often greatly in demand and it is because of this they start to work in these large places.

We would much rather see them go back to smaller venues and reach more people than they are able to the way they work now. Some of them, it has to be said, are not working for the good though. They have been carried away by their own success and are now charging huge sums of money for people to go and see them. This is wrong. If the charges are kept low, you know they are still pure of heart, if the ticket price is far too high, then maybe they have lost their way a little.

We think by now you have got the message we wish to impart. Keep the meetings smaller rather than too large and allow us to guide you where you should be going and how you should be working. Churches, halls, small theatres, private homes, public meeting rooms are all fine. Save the stadiums for sport and concerts. Save the huge theatres for big theatre productions. We are not here to put on an act to impress people, we are here to work and that is what you are meant to be doing with us also.

Remember, you may be called on at any time to do this work. When out for dinner, at a theatre watching a show or on the beach and any other place you can think of. If there is someone where you happen to be who needs an urgent message, we shall ask you to pass it on. This is not going to be often, but from time to time it will be necessary. We will never ask you to do anything at an inappropriate time. There is no more to say on this matter, but we now wish to talk to you about trust.

CHAPTER NINETEEN

Trust
This chapter talks not only of trust between both medium and helper, but also of those who go to them for help

A medium has to be able to have absolute trust in their helpers or guides. So too do we helpers need to be able to place trust in our mediums. Much is at stake when we work together not least of all the reputation of mediumship or healing in general. For those who have worked and studied under us for many years that trust will have built up between us all. It wouldn't have been there at the start and trust would have had to be earned by both sides over a period of time like any relationship.

We know who we are to work with from the moment that person is born and sometimes will have to wait patiently over many of your earth years until the time is right. Once our medium starts to become aware and develop their mediumship skills much patience is required as mistakes are made quite often in the early stages. This can be due to the medium's inability to tune in so well at first to what it is we are trying to communicate to them. Sometimes their own thoughts can intrude into what we are trying to tell them but with experience this is overcome.

So too it is with those of the spirit world who are trying to communicate for the first time. Not all are experienced at this either and we too have to learn how to communicate with those of you we are to work with. These are the stages where trust will be built up gradually. It is the early mistakes made at the start which will make you doubt our sincerity and truthfulness at times. This is understandable and should not be worried over too much. It does mean that you will have to be more vigilant though as this is when discernment will need to be used.

The early days of a medium learning and honing their skills is when they are more open to being used by those less scrupulous spirits who are mischievous. It is never anything serious, but will lead to untruths being given to them in order to deceive and sometimes cause upset. Those who persevere through these early stages and act sensibly and with care will come through that and learn the differences. It is not something that will happen quickly as there is much to learn during the early years. Yes, it takes years. This is not something that is developed very quickly if it is to be done properly. The best mediums have been taught by us over many years indeed. In fact, they still learn until the day they pass into our world to join us. There is not one living person who knows everything although many believe they do.

The other trust needed is between the medium or healer and the ones or ones who come to them for help. Those people put tremendous trust in the healers or mediums and expect honesty and integrity from them. Sadly, they do not always get that. We are thankful that most people working with us are doing so in an honest way. Like all things in life though, there are exceptions. By having read this book we hope you will now be more able to judge who the honest ones are that act with integrity and the ones you should try to avoid.

There is no need for anyone to see a medium regularly. There are some people who want to go every week or month and this is not right. There is no real need for this. If someone tries to come too often, then there is a danger that they will become too dependant on the medium and will not be able to live their lives normally. A medium who acts responsibly would discourage this behaviour and not allow it. There are some though who are more than happy to see people as often as they like. This is because they are paid for their services each time and they are happy to take the money. Those mediums are the ones who have lost their integrity and are not working with the humility required. They are not putting your needs first.

A healer will possibly see the person who comes for help a little more often. Sometimes only one visit will be needed, but for more serious things or recurring problems they may need more visits. Over a period of years, most mediums will find the same people coming back to them for either mediumship or healing. This may not always be for them but could be for or with members of their family or friends. It is over these years that a trust will develop and grow.

Sadly, there are many people who have no trust in healers or mediums. This is due to dreadful stories and experiences they have either experienced themselves or heard about from others. These are the ones who we need to show that there is honesty and integrity in our work. We need to gain their trust and show them that what we do is real and not in the minds of a few. We will only be able to gain their trust and the trust of others by improving the standards of our work in the ways we have spoken of in this book. There is no need to talk more of this now but we would like to talk to you a little more seriously on the matter of your world.

CHAPTER TWENTY

Your world

We talk here about the matters and conditions of your world, mankind and what is happening.

The world that you live in today is in a very bad way and sadly, most of that is due to mankind. You have been given a wonderful place in which to live and yet you all abuse it. Why do you do this? We have already said that the world is becoming a Godless society and this is what causes most of what you see today throughout your world.

You wonder why so many things happen naturally that you call disasters. They are to bring attention to you all that what you do is wrong. The way you live is so bad today. Greed is the worst thing in your lives. This one thing rules so many people in the world. Religious leaders, politicians and governments alike are all just as guilty. The wars and battles caused throughout the world are mainly caused by greed.

There are those who try to say that the world leaders are not doing anything wrong and that the problem lies within the various religions. This is not so. There is no problem with religion. It is sadly many of the people within these religions who say what they do is in the name of whichever faith they believe in. This then is not religion. It is the fanatics within these religions who are the problem. The leaders are not strong enough today and do not stand up and defend their faith. They need to stand firm and state what they believe in and what behaviour they expect of their followers.

This is not a book about religion but we cannot ignore some of what is going on in your world today. So much of what is done in the name of spirituality comes under this banner and therefore it has to be broached. All religions should be respected no matter what their belief system. If what that religion teaches is goodness then it cannot be wrong. What is wrong is that many people within a certain faith do not follow that faith correctly. They change what suits them and yet still claim to be a follower. This is not so and this is what should be stopped.

The leaders of all the religions need to stand and make obvious to one and all what is acceptable belief in their faith and what isn't. They need to be stronger than they are. Too many are afraid to offend another. Why should your belief offend others? If they don't believe in it they have no need to follow it but they should respect you. They don't respect you because you don't respect yourselves.

The political leaders and governments of the world are the main culprits in this war of the world. They are full of greed and corruption. There is no country in the world free of those two things. They are just in varying degrees. The people in those countries, which are developed, are full of greed also. They are never satisfied with what they have. They want more and more and will kill in order to get it. The world is in a terrible state and you are all guilty of allowing this to happen.

How many of you who read this book are living with just the very basics of what you need? It is acceptable for those who have more money than others to live a slightly more luxurious lifestyle as these are changes, which are necessary in the world. Nothing can be exactly the same otherwise experiences and lessons would never happen. What is wrong is when those with more gloat and still moan they do not have enough. They do not help others in need unless it is seen by others that they do it. The more you are all given the more you all want. It is this that brings about the fighting and the wars you see in your world today. It all stems with mans greed.

Many of those who are not so corrupt and try to lead proper lives ask why there is so much in the world today that is bad. It is for this very reason. Those of you who see this and try to lead good lives are in the minority today. You are the ones who we rely on to help us to save the world. It may be very small things that you do, but by your very nature you are doing more than you realise.

They talk of the end of the world and question when this might be and how it shall happen. Do they not realise that it is they who are bringing this about? The way they treat the world given to them and abuse it destroys all around them. Disaster shall follow disaster. War will follow war. Countries will destroy each other and all in them. Sickness and disease shall be rife. Diseases that man shall be unable to treat or cure shall grow and spread throughout the world. All of this and more shall be given to those who are abusing what God gave them.

Sadly, many of those who lead a good life will have to suffer alongside those who destroy the world today. It is unavoidable that this shall happen but their rewards are to be great where they follow.

There are many of you in the world today who are aware of these things already and it is you who we talk to now. You are the ones who are to help us to correct these ways. You might think that this is an impossible task but it isn't. Everything has to start somewhere and you all need to lead by example. We are to spread the word and try to reach as many of you as possible in order to aid this work. It is by using instruments such as we work with now that will allow this to be done.

Our word shall spread and those of you who lead the life we ask shall be instrumental in making these changes start. It is to be an enormous task ahead of you all and shall be very hard indeed. We shall open doors for you in order that your voices may be heard, as we need to start this work now if the world as you know it is to be spared.

Natural disasters are growing in magnitude in order to make people sit and think about how they live now. There have been many all quite close together and now the world rests a little while. Many more disasters are to follow though and some shall be of great magnitude and shall be very close together in order to shock. This will continue until man starts to rethink how he lives today. It is the ordinary man who shall be responsible for changing the ways of their own countries. They shall make their leaders listen to them.

This cannot happen over a short period of time as you will be aware. It has to start somewhere though and now is the time for this. Lead good lives, lead by example and do not strive for more than you need. Be grateful for what you have as there are many with nothing and yet they are content. All of this work that we shall do together is to take longer than your lifetime, but it starts now.

There is a rapid growth of those of you who are aware of the spiritual things and it is you who will be responsible for these changes to start. You must go about your work now and do it well. You must all work in the ways we teach in order for this to be achieved. Word is to spread throughout the world of the ways this can be done and we are to use many instruments in order for this to happen. You all can be of great help to us in spreading the word in how our work should be done. We want to see changes starting to happen as soon as possible.

The world and its problems are not going to be so easy to change. There is a badness that has crept into your world, which is to be very difficult to erase completely. It is to take a very long time indeed and until the ones who lead the worst lives are gone, this is not to be possible. The changes in how one lives can start now though.

We need you to spread the word about how lives should be led. Disasters are to spread throughout until people start to change the way they live now. One after the other will be seen until you all come to see that it is the error of your ways that causes these things. Help is at hand should you wish for it. You do have to listen to what is being said though.

There have been many books before this that have tried to teach the multitudes how they should be living but they are disregarded by most. The ones we talk of are used by world religions and like this book have been written by instruments of that time. They too were inspired by another and dictated to many who put their words together to make one teaching manual. This one is no different in its own way. It too is a teaching manual, which is in order to help bring back the lifestyle that once was.

To live more simply is how one can start. Sharing what you have with others less fortunate. Help where help is needed; care where care should be given. Look after one another. Too many people in your world today ignore their responsibilities and push them onto others. Most are too busy living their lives selfishly to care what happens to others in their lives. This must change. The way of change is with the disasters of the world.

Each time a major disaster is unleashed upon the world it brings out the best in humans. The peace and caring that unfolds is wonderful to behold. Sadly, this is very short lived as their memories are also. This is why more natural disasters of God's hands shall be unleashed on the world to teach that what they do is wrong. Man is destroying what was given to him and he must be brought to task if the world is to be saved.

No more of this for now, but you have been forewarned of what is to be expected unless ways are changed drastically. Those of you who work with us are to be instrumental in helping bring those changes about. We ask you now to work well together and in the ways we teach you.

No one of you is better than another. Each person born into your world is equal and it is only by his or her free will that they become what they do. We talk not of material goods we talk of their hearts and souls. Lessons are to be learned through many lifetimes and there are those who choose not to learn or progress for good. They are too caught up with the materialism of your world and do not wish to change that. Theirs is the worst lot to have and are to be pitied.

Not all with great wealth are of this state of mind. There are those who have much and do many good things for others that is not heard of. They are pure of heart and use what they have in order to try and help as many as they can. They are well blessed indeed as are those of you who give of yourself to others.

Have faith our friends as to have no faith means you have no hope in your life. All should believe in something greater than themselves. It is sad that so many think there is nothing but the here and now of the world they live in. We are proof that this is not so. If only they took the time to think about those things that man is unable to make or provide for you that you need for your very existence. They refuse to listen. They refuse to open their hearts or minds. They are the ones who are the most poor no matter what worldly goods they posses.

Those of you who believe in something or someone far greater than yourselves or your world are the richest. You are the ones who put your trust elsewhere. To trust and have blind faith is truly a wonderful gift in itself. You are the ones who please us and who we are able to place our trust in, in return.

With the help of this teaching manual and all others that have been written in a similar vein we hope to change the world to a better place for one and all. We hope to change it to what it was meant to be. The choice is yours to make. All we can do is help to show you the way it can be done. This is one way we can help guide you. It is not as your real guides work but by other means. Together we are able to change much and we thank you for listening to us and helping as we are sure most of you shall. Read the Holy books that have gone before it matters not which. They all speak the same language, which is the language of peace and good living. This is what we try to teach also. Every race, religion, man or woman must all work together for the greater good. Ignore your differences, look at your similarities and work on those.

CHAPTER TWENTY-ONE

Conclusion
A brief summary

There is not much more for us to say in this book, as we are to follow in time with others. This was but a start to try to teach you the correct way for things to be done. We realise that all must be allowed to learn in whatever way they choose and they all have their own path to follow. It is only a wish we have that makes us write this book in order that you might be prepared to listen.

There are those who shall and many more who shall not. This is something we are well aware of and which saddens us. It matters not though, as each has their own path to tread and eventually they shall all come to the same conclusion if intended for them.

There are those who will say that we have left out some very pertinent bits in this book. Those being mainly card reading, crystal ball gazing, scrying and many other means of divination. We have omitted these deliberately as we do not normally work with such things. These to us are mere superstitious ways of working and are not the ways we intend for this work to be done.

A true medium will never work in this way and those who do use some form of divination usually only do so in order to focus their minds. They may use some form of this to work psychically initially, but will soon move from this to working purely with the spirit world. Those who work solely with any of the things we have mentioned above are not mediums. They are what the people of your world call fortune-tellers.

It is these people who usually charge the most money and give the least genuine information. Many people who live by superstition and who have no real belief system in their lives seek after these fortune-tellers greatly in your world. There is no doubt that they too offer a service for many where it is needed. It is just not the way things are intended to be done. Please do not confuse this work or these people with mediumship and the work of the spirit world.

There are many clairvoyants who work genuinely with the intention of helping to guide and give hope to those they read for. They will be working psychically and actually have no real need for any of these things. It does help them to focus though, and those they read for like to see something that looks like work is being done. The ones we decry are those who are total frauds and tell generalisations to those poor souls who come to them in desperation seeking help and guidance. What they do to mislead them is wicked and one day they shall have to answer for these misdeeds.

Lotions, potions and the like are all useless to anyone working in these fields and those who say they aren't are deluding themselves and those who believe them. If they wish to believe it and it brings them hope and comfort then so be it. We just do not wish those of you who are reading this to confuse those ways of working with the true world of spirit. We would never work in such ways and have no need to.

This also brings us to the subject of physical mediumship and trance work. Those who talk of physical mediumship are mainly those who again like to see dramatic things happen in front of them. They are the ones who lack true faith and therefore, shall not believe unless they see. It is like doubting Thomas who is spoken of in the Bible. He too could not believe unless he saw. This is what you are like. It is totally unnecessary for any form of trickery to be undertaken for this work to be done. Tilting tables, Ouija boards, moving objects and the like are done for demonstration purposes, which we liken to a circus act.

Why are some in spirit made to perform in this way? Those who undertake this and partake of it are encouraging the lower energy forms who love to play these games. They are not the ones who work in the highest sense of this work. This is something we would like to see stopped. Should we ever do any of those things it will be in private and for a specific purpose. It is rarely done and there is no need for it. It is strictly for those who are not serious about the real works of our world.

Those who need specific proof of our existence by playing these party tricks as we call them are the very people we would like to see discouraged from undergoing this work. The ones who encourage them to partake of it are even worse in our eyes. They are meant to be the experienced mediums and teachers. As such, they should know better than to play in this way. As we have said many times throughout this book, mediumship is a very serious way of working and must be done with the utmost humility. There is nothing humble about showing off in this way. Please do not go to any of these demonstrations and please try wherever you can to discourage them from being done.

We are aware that these practices and many like them will continue to go on, but this is exactly what causes ridicule in our work. This is why we strive to seek those of your world who are of pure heart and humble to work with us. Those who wish to work in a way that denounces all of these strange rituals and behaviour patterns are the ones who we need to be working with in order to raise the standards of true mediumship.

Those of you who learn today are to be instrumental in helping us to achieve this. Those who are still reading this book must surely be in agreement with all that we say to you and will also help us in our endeavours. The harder we all work together the quicker we can change the way things are today. We can start by doing what has been spoken of in this book. You can help us by becoming the leaders in this important work.

We work very hard indeed to be able to reach those of you who are able to communicate with us and we wish our work to be acknowledged and supported. We do this work to benefit those of your world who need support and hope. We do it together with you in order that you might be aware that there is a world beyond yours which is better for one and all. We do not need to do this work, we choose to. You too have no need to do this work with us. In fact, there are many who have been chosen who do walk away from it.

It is up to us all to stop the practices, which are undertaken today in the wrong way or have them changed. Most who do these things the wrong way are unaware that they do so. We hope that by relating what we have to you all you will listen and see what we say to you is correct. Please take the time to think about what we have told you and the reasoning behind it all. It has not been said to denounce you all, nor has it been said to cause offence. It has been said in order that your work and ours can at last be accepted and respected by everyone of your world. We can only expect this to happen when all the strange rituals and behavioural problems have been controlled or stopped.

We do hope that you have enjoyed reading this small book which we have written with the help of our instrument and that it will be beneficial to one and all. No doubt, you will wish to know who we are that tell you all of this. Our names are not important but we are aware that a name has to be given in order for this book to be published and sold if our work is to be recognised and taken seriously. It is very hard for us to do this as we have already stated to you that names are not at all necessary where we are now but we give a name to you which we feel will help in our work. This name is to be Zeduchial. It is more than one of us who has been with our instrument whilst this work was being done, but she is aware of who Zeduchial is and it is, therefore, most appropriate that this is the name that shall be used for our works should one be needed.

As we have told you, there will be more booklets or manuals to follow this introductory one but they will be focused on teaching you the individual ways that our work should be done to our liking. It will not be too long before the first of these shall follow, but first we allow this book to be published and read by as many as possible in order that any following lessons we have for you will be widely accepted and read also.

We thank you for being patient with us and reading what we had to say to you. We again say that we have no wish to offend anyone by what we say. Every person has a right to their own beliefs and we above all respect them as we hope they too will respect us and those who work with us. We wish you well in your work and look forward to working with many of you who are reading this now. We are aware who already does this with us and who shall be in the future. We are also aware of those of you who are in need of changing from the old ways to the ones we teach you here. We ask you please to consider what we have said and hope that you will be enthusiastic and serious enough about this work that you shall heed what we have had to tell you.

Our blessings go to each and every one of you and may God's Holy Light shine upon you one and all. May those who need help or healing receive that which they need in order to lead a peaceful and happy life. Be assured that your own special angel is there with you every second, minute and hour throughout the whole of your lives in order to guide you and guard you whether you believe or not. If you can believe in the angels then that belief will bring you the comfort and the hope that you seek.

Remember, you are never alone. Even in your darkest moments they are with you. Just ask and they will help. Trust in them and they will never let you down. Things do not always happen and prayers are not always answered in the way you wish for, but be assured that the outcome shall always be in your best interest. Even if you are not aware how it could be at the time, at a later date you will understand and be truly thankful. We in the world of spirit send our love and thanks to you all and your angel stands by you at all times. Peace be with all of you in your daily lives. God Bless you all.

Final note from the author

You might remember reading the following section at the beginning of **A Guide's Guide**, I have put it here again for you now as I tell you what has happened to me since finishing writing this book back in 2009.

Excerpt from start of the book:

...The spirit world is most grateful to those who help us to continue our work and we, in turn, wish to help them. That then is the reason for this book to be written.

The one we use to write this for us is herself now learning and is almost ready to work with us. She has, in fact already done many things but has yet to develop the full potential she is capable of. That is soon to follow after this manual is completed.

She is not at all responsible for the contents of this book and we use her only to pass what we need to tell you on to everyone. We are most grateful to her also for allowing us to use her in this way...

This book was intended to be my first ever book. It was put on a writing site called Authonomy and was spotted by someone who suggested I contact Literary Agents they thought would be interested. I had only written the first couple of chapters and there was no introduction as there is now. I had written those words 5 years earlier and they had sat in a drawer at my home ever since.

After seeing what I had written to date, the agents asked for my whole manuscript. I didn't have a whole manuscript! I asked for two weeks to 'tidy it up' and set to work writing. This whole book was written in that two weeks and needed no editing apart from the bits I wrote myself in the introduction.

They state above that my work with them is to start soon after completion of this book. It did. In the last year, my agents have had this book and so nothing has happened with it. In the meantime, I have started two blogs, one which is spiritual and talks of things spiritual as well as being instructional, I have started a site for authors where we help promote each other, I have self-published two books which are spiritual compilations whilst people waited for this to be published, have completed one other besides and am in the process of writing a couple of others.

Apart from all of that, I am now a public speaker, do photographic readings from photographs online for people throughout the world and have started to help others to develop their full potential also. All of this has happened in just over twelve months. You tell me the spirit world isn't at work here. I just hope they are right and open the doors they say they shall for this book to be read throughout the world.

Where to see more of Lorraine and how to contact her:

E-mail

lorraine@authorsonshow.com
or
lvg@blueyonder.co.uk

Private Blogs:

A Sceptical Medium
http://askamedium.wordpress.com/
Lorraine – The Blog
http://bitly5z1ezq.blogspot.com/

Writing Blogs:

Authors on Show
http://authorsonshow.com/
AOS
http://authorsonshow.blogspot.com/

Printed in Great Britain
by Amazon.co.uk, Ltd.,
Marston Gate.